READING
Rehearsing and Exploring the Standards

We're all about st...

ISBN 978-1-5166-1996-2
R 1996-2

Contents

*Literary (L), Informational (I), and Paired Passages
with Multiple Choice, Short Response, Extended Response, and Essay Questions*

Introduction

Reading: Rehearsing and Exploring the Standards is an instruction-based book which prepares students for success on the types of reading tasks and assessments they will encounter in school.

This instruction-based book provides students with a variety of question types as well as an organized review of how to answer these questions. Featured are authentic and complex passages, focusing on close reading and using text-based complex questions that require students to analyze, critique, and make connections.

There are four units in each book:
• Part A: Key Ideas and Details
• Part B: Craft and Structure
• Part C: Integration of Knowledge and Ideas
• Part D: All Together

Each unit begins with an Instruction section that features one informational and one literary passage. The blue bar on every page contains guides that help students focus on important details and answer questions about the text. The All Together unit allows students to utilize the skills they learned and complete questions on their own.

Question types include:
• Multiple Choice
• Short Response
• Extended Response
• Essay Questions

Graphic organizers are included with each passage to help students organize their work.

The book contains both literary and informational passages, and several sets of paired passages. Each passage or set of passages is followed by 15 questions, which cover all the standards.

Part A:

Key Ideas and Details

Literary and Informational Passages with Multiple Choice, Short Response, Extended Response, and Essay Questions

Reading Standards

R.4.1   Refer to details and examples in a text when explaining what the text says explicitly and when drawing inferences from the text.

   ✓ **Informational**   ✓ **Literary**

R.4.2   Determine the main idea of a text and explain how it is supported by key details; summarize the text. Determine a theme of a story, drama, or poem from details in the text; summarize the text.

   ✓ **Informational**   ✓ **Literary**

R.4.3   Explain events, procedures, ideas, or concepts in a historical, scientific, or technical text, including what happened and why, based on specific information in the text. Describe in depth a character, setting, or event in a story or drama, drawing on specific details in the text (e.g., a character's thoughts, words, or actions).

   ✓ **Informational**   ✓ **Literary**

Instruction

Directions: Read the passage. The guides in the blue bar will help you focus on some of the important details. Then answer the questions that follow. These questions will also have guides to help you find the correct answers.

Doodlebug and Dandelion: When Turkeys Fly

By Pamela Dell
Art by Dom Mansell

Look at the title. Look at the illustrations. What do you think this passage will be about?

1   "I'LL BE UPSTAIRS if you need me," Mrs. Bogsworth announced to her son Boggington Bogsworth the Third and his two best friends, Doodlebug and Dandelion Pinkley. "I'm so proud of you kids. Making a whole Thanksgiving dinner isn't easy."

2   "No sweat, Mom," Bog said. "Go finish grading your papers. We got it covered."

3   "We'll follow your instructions exactly," Dandelion promised.

4   Mrs. Bogsworth had spent the morning giving them lessons in gaxtro-cooking, a strange, science-based way of making food. The turkey was in the oven. Now the kids would use what they'd learned to make the other dishes.

5   Mrs. Bogsworth wasn't actually a chef. She taught high school science. Bog's dad, Brogue Bogsworth the Second, was an airline pilot. But their kitchen had as many modern cooking gadgets as a restaurant.

6 "Watch the time," Mrs. Bogsworth said. "Our guests arrive at four o'clock. And, weather willing, your dad will be on time, too, Bog." She crossed her fingers, smiled, and left.

7 "This will be great!" Dandelion looked eagerly at the huge kitchen island stacked with utensils and ingredients.

When do you think this story takes place?

8 "We'll show 'em how it's done, right, Dandelion?" Bog said, beginning his first recipe.

9 All this time, Doodlebug had said nothing. He loved food. He even thought cooking could be fun. But he wasn't at all sure what he was doing there. He stared at the list of dishes and tried to remember Mrs. Bogsworth's instructions. Finally, he picked one. But Dandelion had beat him to it. She was busy turning cheese and bananas into a yummy-looking foam to decorate the pumpkin soup.

10 "Wait," Doodlebug said, "I was going to make that one!"

11 "You snooze, you lose!" Dandelion retorted, elbowing him away.

12 Grumbling, Doodlebug chose another. But just then Bog grabbed the tube of lemon curd and squeezed it into a mixer with fish paste and peanut butter crackers to make stuffing.

13 "I could make that," Doodlebug offered.

14 "Too late," Bog grinned. "This one's mine, and it's gonna be righteous!"

15 "Yummmm!" Dandelion exclaimed, pushing Doodlebug away once again. "Everything smells great!" She had just made a heap of edible paper from potatoes and soybeans to wrap chocolate-covered olives in.

What is unique about the food the children are making?

16 Bog had turned olive oil into powder and was sprinkling it on his Brussels-sprouts-and-marmalade pie. His whole face was covered with the stuff.

17 Doodlebug had had enough of Bog and Dandelion hogging all the good cooking chores. "I'm making the mashed pickles and snail gravy!" he roared, getting to work before they could take over.

18 A while later, Mrs. Bogsworth shouted from upstairs, "Almost four o'clock, chefs!"

19 Dandelion gasped. Bog groaned. Doodlebug said, "Weren't we supposed to take the turkey out before now?"

20 Dandelion and Bog looked horror-struck. By now it had to be over-done. And they'd pumped the turkey full of Mega-helium, a special gas to make it more plump and flavorful.

21 "Hurry!" Dandelion screeched, just as the doorbell rang.

22 "Careful when you open the oven door, Bog…" Doodlebug said—but not soon enough.

23 Bog had already grabbed the handle and pulled. Instantly, a super-plump turkey exploded from the oven and shot toward the ceiling. It was airborne!— but still barely cooked. You could clearly see its goosebumped flesh.

What is wrong with the turkey when it shoots out of the oven?

24 The kids screamed and reached wildly for the bird. But just before it hit the ceiling, the turkey did a loop-de-loop and shot sideways, barely missing a window. Next, it dropped low and roared by just above their heads. Still screaming, everyone ducked, barely escaping a direct hit.

25 Finally, the turkey did one last out-of-control spin in the air and flopped to the floor with a wet SPLAT! sound. At that moment, Mrs. Bogsworth charged into the kitchen with the guests following—Uncle Bongo Bogsworth the Fourth, Aunt Selina, and the Pinkley parents.

26 "What the dickens?!" Mrs. Bogsworth cried.

27 The three kids stared guiltily at the floor.

28 Then, to their surprise, Mr. Bogsworth appeared. Knowing all about gaxtro-cooking, he understood the situation immediately and burst out laughing.

29 "Dad, you're home!" Bog said, giving him a big hug.

30 "I think we used too much gas," Dandelion whispered, eyeing the bird as if afraid it was still alive.

31 Doodlebug said nothing, glad his kitchen time was over.

32 Mr. Bogsworth looked pleased. "When I landed, a foul-looking goose sat itself on my windshield and gave me a nasty evil eye. So I won't miss eating turkey at all!"

What does Mr. Bogsworth say about the turkey failure?

33 "Thanksgiving dinner's a great success!" Mrs. Bogsworth praised, ushering everyone to the dining room.

34 As he dug into the delicious gaxtro dishes, Doodlebug sighed with relief. Forget cooking food. He just wanted to eat.

10

1 Which character is a high school science teacher?

A Mr. Bogsworth

B Doodlebug

C Mrs. Bogsworth

D Dandelion

This is a **Facts and Details** question. Where in the passage does it talk about the characters' jobs?

---

2 Read the following lines from the passage:

> *"Wait," Doodlebug said, "I was going to make that one!"*

> *"You snooze, you lose!" Dandelion retorted, elbowing him away.*

> *Grumbling, Doodlebug chose another.*

Which word best describes how Doodlebug feels here?

A relieved

B frustrated

C happy

D sorry

This is a **Character** question. You can read the words around these lines to better understand the situation and why Doodlebug feels the way he does.

---

3 Which of the following is a theme, or main idea, of this passage?

A Money often causes more problems than it is worth.

B Parents should not let children cook.

C People should always do things the same way.

D Sometimes people should take risks and try new things.

This is a **Main Idea** question. The theme, or main idea, is a message that describes an overall lesson the characters learn in the story.

4 Why did Bog and Dandelion look horror-struck at one point?

(A) They were afraid the turkey had been cooking for too long.

B They were afraid that their parents would find out what they had done.

C They thought that what Doodlebug said was funny.

D They realized that it was late and they needed to go home.

> This is a **Character** question. What happens in the story's plot to make Bog and Dandelion look and feel this way?

5 Why did Mr. Bogsworth not want to eat turkey?

A He had never liked turkey.

B When he was a kid, he had a pet turkey, so he did not eat them.

C He was a vegetarian.

(D) A mean-looking goose had landed on his windshield earlier.

> This is a **Facts and Details** question. Look back in the passage to understand Mr. Bogsworth's reasoning.

6 Why is Mrs. Bogsworth upstairs?

A She is taking a nap.

(B) She is grading papers.

C She does not know how to cook.

D She does not like turkeys.

> This is a **Character** question. How is Mrs. Bogsworth feeling? What is her reasoning for going upstairs?

7 Which of the following did the kids produce?

A tomato soup

B a dandelion-flavored drink

C edible paper

D fried goose

This is a **Facts and Details** question. Look back in the passage for some examples of the children's whacky recipes.

8 Did Mrs. Bogsworth seem to trust Bog, Doodlebug, and Dandelion or not? Explain, giving details from the story to support your answer.

This is a **Character** question. How do you think Mrs. Bogsworth feels about these characters from reading the passage?

9 What does gaxtro-cooking seem to be? Explain, providing details from the story to support your answer.

This is a **Facts and Details** question. Based upon what the children are doing in the passage text, what do you think this term means?

10 Explain what happens to the turkey and how each character reacts. Use details from the story to support your answer.

This is a **Character** question. Reread the passage to see how each character reacts to certain events in this story.

11 Why might Doodlebug have been "glad his kitchen time was over"? Use details from the story to support your answer.

This is a **Character** question. How do the other characters seem to treat Doodlebug throughout this story?

12 At one point, Dandelion says, "This will be great!" Why does he say that? Use details from the story to support your answer.

This is a **Character** question. How do you think Dandelion feels when he says this?

13 Why might this story be titled: "Doodlebug and Dandelion: When Turkeys Fly"?

This is a **Main Idea** question. You are searching for the main idea, or theme behind the title.

14 Choose two characters. Describe their relationship, providing support from the passage for your answers.

Planning Space
You can write notes, make a list, or draw a chart to help plan your answer.

This is a **Story Relationship/Character** question. It is your job to pick two characters and explain how they are related to each other throughout this passage.

_____

_____

_____

_____

_____

_____

_____

_____

_____

_____

_____

15 List and explain the steps that happen with the turkey from the beginning to the end of the passage.

This is a **Story Connections** question. You need to search for the various events that occur in the plot of this story, then piece them together from start to finish.

Planning Space

Use the flow chart below to list the steps.

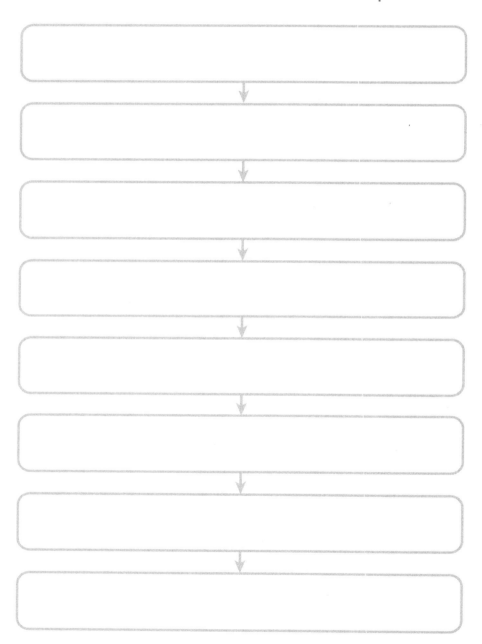

_____

_____

_____

_____

_____

_____

_____

_____

_____

_____

_____

_____

Directions: Read the passage. The guides in the blue bar will help you focus on some of the important details. Then answer the questions that follow. These questions will also have guides to help you find the correct answers.

Do Forests Need Fires?

Art by Amanda Shepherd

Look at the title. Look at the illustration. What do you think this passage will be about?

1   Fire is nothing to mess with. Uncontrolled, it can be dangerous, destructive, and scary. And forest fires are about the scariest. What could be worse for trees than fire?

1. Dead leaves, twigs, and fallen trees build up over many years.

2. Lightning strikes! The intense heat starts a fire.

3. Animals flee to safe places or hide underground.

4. After the fire, ash enriches the soil.

2   Yet though they are terrifying to see, forest fires are a natural part of forest life. They can even help keep the forest healthy. Fire clears away underbrush and nourishes the soil. It makes open spaces for young trees to grow and clears the way for sun-loving shrubs that provide food and homes for many animals.

3   Fire also helps keep pests in check. <u>Disease and insects kill more trees each year than fire does.</u> A healthy burn destroys these threats. Though a fire will kill some trees, many survive, protected by thick bark. Most old trees have lived through many fires. Some trees even need the heat of a fire to open their seed pods.

What is a much bigger threat to forest trees than fire?

Fire in the Forest

Even when a big fire burns the forest to the ground, amazing things follow. Within months, new plants start to grow.

5. Wildflowers spring up in the new sunny places.

6. In a year or two, grass and shrubs move in.

7. New sun-loving trees sprout. Soon they shade out the grass and shrubs.

8. Eventually a new shady forest grows— until the next fire.

4   As foresters learn more about how fire helps forests, they are changing the way they fight forest and prairie fires. Instead of trying to put out every fire, they now often let natural fires (sparked by heat or lightning) burn. They've learned that letting small fires clear up the dry brush lowers the risk of a really big fire that could get out of control.

5   Of course, it's still important to put out unnatural fires that people start or that get too near homes or towns. Firefighters dig trenches, dump water, and even set fires of their own to try to control a fire's path. Friend or foe, fire is always something to respect.

What sort of fires do firefighters fight that are NOT found in forests?

Firefi

1 Which statement best summarizes the passage?

   A All forest fires are bad for the environment.

   B Many benefits come from natural forest fires.

   C Some old trees have survived many fires.

   D Twigs build up over many years.

This is a **Main Idea** question. In informational passages, a summary is a brief explanation of what a particular piece of the passage (or the whole passage) is about.

2 Which sentence from the passage best supports the idea that forest fires help destroy pests? –Bugs

   A "Fire is nothing to mess with."

   B "A healthy burn destroys those threats."

   C "After the fire, ash enriches the soil."

   D "Friend or foe, fire is always something to respect."

This is a **Facts and Details** question. The question is giving you the idea. Look at the choices and choose the best one that supports this idea.

3 Which of the following kills the fewest trees each year?

   A bugs

   B deer

   C insects

   D fires

This is a **Facts and Details** question. The answer to this question can be discovered by rereading the passage.

4 After a fire, around how long does it take for shrubs and grass to grow?

   A five days

   B six to eight months

   C one or two years

   D around 35 years

This is a **Facts and Details** question. Look back in the passage to discover how long a new shrub or grass takes to grow.

5 Which of the following is not mentioned as something that firefighters do to stop some forest fires?

A setting other fires

B digging trenches

C leaving the area

D putting water on them

This is an **Events in Text** question. Firefighters have procedures to put out forest fires, based on details in the passage. Which of these is not listed?

6 What inference can you make about this author's attitude towards forest fires?

A The author feels negatively.

B The author feels uncaring.

C The author feels angry.

D The author feels positive.

This is a **Facts and Details/Inferences** question. The author doesn't say outright how they feel about forest fires, but how can you tell based on their tone?

7 Why do some trees need the heat that comes from forest fires?

A to allow their seed pods to open

B to protect them from harmful sunlight

C to keep them warm

D to give them nutrients

This is a **Facts and Details** question. Go back in the passage and reread about how trees live through forest fires (and some actually benefit from them!)

8 Why would uncontrolled forest fires be "dangerous, destructive, and scary"? Use details from the passage to support your answer.

This is an **Ideas in Text** question. What about fires specifically would make a fire often have these traits?

_____

_____

_____

_____

_____

_____

_____

_____

_____

_____

9 How does fire help young trees grow? Use details from the passage to support your answer.

This is a **Facts and Details** question. You can reread the passage to discover how fire actually in fact can HELP young trees.

10 How are pests reduced through fire? Why is this important? Use details from the passage to support your answer.

This is an **Ideas in Text** question. Fire naturally reduces pests, and firefighters picked up on this idea while trying to put these fires out. How does fire naturally solve this problem?

11 What are some of the dangers of fires that people set randomly? Use details from the passage to support your answer.

This is a **Facts and Details** question. The end of this passage contains the information about fires set by people.

12 What is the main idea of this passage? Use details from the passage to support your answer.

This is a **Main Idea** question. A **Main Idea** is one explanation of what the entire passage is about.

13 How does the passage explain that some old trees survive forest fires? Use details from the passage to support your answer.

This is a **Facts and Details** question. Reread the passage to discover how an old tree can in fact live through a deadly fire.

14 What have foresters learned about how forests benefit from fire? How has this changed their methods of dealing with fire? Use details from the passage to support your answer.

This is a **Facts and Details** question. You can learn more about foresters and their techniques with fire by reading paragraph 4 of this passage.

Planning Space
You can write notes, make a list, or draw a chart to help plan your answer.

_____

_____

_____

_____

_____

_____

_____

_____

_____

_____

_____

_____

_____

_____

15 Compare and contrast controlled and uncontrolled forest fires.

This is a **Facts and Details** question. How are controlled fires and uncontrolled fires different?

Planning Space

You can complete the chart below to help plan your answer.

Similar Characteristics

Controlled Fires	Uncontrolled Fires

Different Characteristics

Controlled Fires	Uncontrolled Fires

_____

_____

_____

_____

_____

_____

_____

_____

_____

_____

_____

_____

Independent Practice

Directions: Read the poem. Then answer the questions that follow.

The Rain Cloud and the Camel

By Lori Mortensen

1   Said the rain cloud to the camel,
    "Why don't you move away?
    The desert's such a prickly place.
    Why would you want to stay?

2   "Come with me and you will see
    Where dandelions grow,
    Where water sparkles in the streams,
    And gentle breezes blow."

3   Said the camel to the rain cloud,
    "Thanks for stopping by.
    The desert *is* a prickly place
    With seasons long and dry.

4   "But I would rather stay right here,
    Where the sun shines warm and bright,
    Where sandy dunes flow like the sea,
    And stars fill up the night.

5   "Still, as you float through endless skies,"
    Said the camel with a wink,
    "I'm always glad each time you come
    To share a rainy drink."

Directions: Answer the following questions. If you need more space to write an answer, write your answer on your own paper.

1 Which inference do the rain cloud's words in the first stanza best support?

 A   He has never seen a desert before.

 B   He feels sorry for the camel.

 C   He has been all over the world.

 D   He wants to make the camel feel bad.

2 Why does the camel decide to stay in the desert?

 A   He is too afraid to leave.

 B   He thinks the rain cloud is lying.

 C   He can live without water.

 D   He enjoys living there.

3 Which statement best explains how the camel feels about the rain cloud?

 A   He wishes he could float with the rain cloud.

 B   He thinks the rain cloud should stay in the desert.

 C   He enjoys seeing the rain cloud from time to time.

 D   He believes that the rain cloud likes causing trouble.

4 The central message of the poem is about the importance of—

 A   making new friends.

 B   exploring new places.

 C   being happy with what you have.

 D   trying to make your dreams come true.

5 Based on the poem, the reader can infer that the rain cloud—

   A enjoys hot weather.

   B doesn't like the camel.

   C usually comes out at night.

   D doesn't visit the desert often.

6 How does the rain cloud most help the camel?

   A The rain cloud takes the camel away.

   B The rain cloud gives the camel water.

   C The rain cloud shows the camel that the desert is unpleasant.

   D The rain cloud tells the camel about places where flowers grow.

7 Which detail best supports the idea that the camel likes the desert?

   A The camel wants to be where the sun shines.

   B The camel thanks the rain cloud for stopping by.

   C The camel admits that the desert is a prickly place.

   D The camel says the desert seasons are long and dry.

8 Why does the rain cloud call the desert a "prickly place"? Use details from the poem to support your answer.

9 Compare the place the rain cloud describes in the second stanza with a desert. Include at least **two** examples from the poem of how a desert is different.

10 The poem describes a conversation between a rain cloud and a camel. Do you think the conversation would have changed the rain cloud's opinions about living in the desert? Use details from the poem to support your conclusion.

11 The camel knows that the desert has both good and bad points. Complete the chart below to summarize what the camel likes and dislikes about living in the desert.

Life in the Desert

Good Points	Bad Points
1)	1)
2)	2)
3)	3)

12 How would the camel most likely sound when he speaks in the last stanza? Explain how this helps show how the camel feels about the desert. Use details from the poem to support your answer.

13 Read this common saying.

Don't judge a book by its cover.

Which character in the poem does the lesson of this saying most relate to? Explain your choice.

14 In the second stanza, the rain cloud describes a place that he likes. In the fourth stanza, the camel describes a place that he likes. Describe how the language used by each character shows how they feel about the place described. Use specific examples of the language used in each stanza to support your answer.

Planning Space

You can complete the chart below to help plan your answer.

Example of Language in the Second Stanza	What the Language Suggests

Example of Language in the Fourth Stanza	What the Language Suggests

_____

_____

_____

_____

_____

_____

_____

_____

_____

_____

_____

_____

_____

15 How does the poem show the importance of making the most of what you have? Use details from the poem to support your answer.

Planning Space

You can write notes, make a list, or draw a chart to help plan your answer.

_____

_____

_____

_____

_____

_____

_____

_____

_____

_____

_____

_____

_____

Directions: Read the passage. Then answer the questions that follow it.

Dazzling Dave Spins Delight

By Cheryl Weibye Wilke

1   Wherever you see Dazzling Dave, you're likely to see him walk the dog, skin the cat, and split the atom. Dave Schulte is a professional yo-yo performer. He spins about 13,000 yo-yo tricks each year. He performs about 130 shows annually, teaching children around the world how to yo-yo.

2   Dave started to yo-yo when he was in college. "I was stressed out during a week of tests when my neighbor stopped by and said, 'Hey, this will help.' I picked up his yo-yo for relief, but *then* I really wanted to figure it out. It was challenging!"

Yo-Yo Teacher

3   After college, Dave taught middle-school students. But he couldn't get the yo-yo off his mind and out of his hands. So he left teaching to yo-yo full time. Soon, he discovered that he still had a passion for teaching.

4   So Dave became a yo-yo teacher! He teaches how to yo-yo, of course. But he also teaches the fundamentals of physics and why things spin.

5   Dave says the main skill needed to become good at yo-yoing is hand-eye coordination. "Juggling and sports such as baseball and lacrosse are great activities to work on that."

6   When he first started to yo-yo, Dave learned hundreds of new tricks each year. "I was yo-yoing eight hours a day." The first trick Dave remembers really working at was called the Star. It took him two or three days to learn it. Now, he says, "I learn about one new trick a month. But they're super-duper tough tricks."

7   Who's coming up with all the new tricks? "Kids from ages 10 to 16 who are getting into the yo-yo," says Dave, grinning. "One of my biggest challenges is keeping up with the new 'school tricks'— tricks developed almost daily by creative kids who have time to work with the yo-yo."

Yo-Yo Master

8   As in most sports, practice, practice, and more practice does make perfect. Dave is a National Yo-Yo Master. It's the highest honor in this sport. There are only 13 National Yo-Yo Masters in the world. They are chosen for their skill with the yo-yo and for their hard work to promote the yo-yo in their communities. Now that's dazzling!

Do You Yo-Yo?

9   All you need to yo-yo is ... a yo-yo! Dave recommends getting one that unscrews so that you can untangle knots.

10   Once you have selected your yo-yo, customize it to your height. Begin by holding the yo-yo between your feet on the floor. Raise the string and tie an overhand knot level with your belly button. Cut off the excess string. Make a slipknot for the middle finger of your throwing hand. You can go on the Internet to learn how to tie a slipknot. Dave suggests changing the string after four to six hours of yo-yo playing time, or if it's dirty or worn.

11   Finally, Dave recommends joining or forming a yo-yo club. The best way to learn, he says, is hands-on. Go to your public library for books and videos.

Tip

12   Hold the yo-yo in your hand with your palm up. Make sure that the string is looped around your middle finger and goes over the top of the yo-yo.

Got Your Yo-Yo? Now Let's Go!

Here are some neat and easy tricks to learn:

Throwdown

Curl up your arm as if you're making a muscle.

Bring your elbow down with a snap and release the yo-yo as it goes over the ends of your fingers.

Then turn your hand over to catch the yo-yo upon return.

Sleeper

Start with a Throwdown.

Leave the yo-yo spinning at the bottom of the string.

Before it slows down too much, turn your hand over (palm down) and give the string a slight upward jerk to return the yo-yo to your hand.

Walk the Dog

Throw a fast Sleeper. Gently lower the yo-yo to the floor so that it barely touches.

Don't bounce your hand. The yo-yo will begin to move along the floor.

Directions: Answer the following questions. If you need more space to write an answer, write your answer on your own paper.

1 Which sentence best supports the idea that teaching yo-yo involves science?

A "He spins about 13,000 yo-yo tricks each year."

B "He performs about 130 shows annually, teaching children around the world how to yo-yo."

C "But he also teaches the fundamentals of physics and why things spin."

D "Dave says the main skill needed to become good at yo-yoing is hand-eye coordination."

2 What is the main purpose of the information in paragraph 2?

A to explain one of the main benefits of using yo-yos

B to describe how Dave got started using a yo-yo

C to warn that learning the yo-yo is difficult at first

D to suggest that people of all ages can enjoy yo-yoing

3 Which sentence from the article helps readers understand the phrases "walk the dog," "skin the cat," and "split the atom"?

A "He spins about 13,000 yo-yo tricks each year."

B "But he also teaches the fundamentals of physics and why things spin."

C "As in most sports, practice, practice, and more practice does make perfect."

D "There are only 13 National Yo-Yo Masters in the world."

4 Which sentence supports the idea that you need eye-hand coordination to become good at yo-yoing?

A "I picked up this yo-yo for relief, but then I really wanted to figure it out."

B "Juggling and sports such as baseball and lacrosse are great activities to work on that."

C "When he first started to yo-yo, Dave learned hundreds of new tricks each year."

D "Finally, Dave recommends joining or forming a yo-yo club."

5 Why does Dave recommend getting a yo-yo that unscrews?

A They spin better than other yo-yos.

B They can be taken apart to untangle knots.

C They are easier to adjust to different heights.

D They are used by professional yo-yo teachers.

6 When adjusting a yo-yo to your height, what should you do right before cutting off the excess string?

A Raise the string.

B Hold the yo-yo between your feet on the floor.

C Tie an overhand knot level with your belly button.

D Make a slipknot for the middle finger of your throwing hand.

7 How do the tricks explained in the "Got Your Yo-Yo? Now Let's Go!" section relate to one another?

A Each trick builds on the one before it.

B All the tricks can be learned very quickly.

C All the tricks require use of a special yo-yo.

D Each trick begins with a different approach.

8 In the first sentence, what do the terms "walk the dog," "skin the cat," and "split the atom" refer to? Use details from the article to support your answer.

9 The article describes how Dave yo-yos as a career. Has Dave been successful in his career? Use at least **two** details from the article to support your answer.

10 Use details from the article to support the conclusion that yo-yoing well requires patience. Use at least **two** details from the article in your answer.

11 How are the tricks Dave learns today different from the tricks he learned when he first started? Describe at least **two** differences in your answer.

12 What is the main idea of the sub-section "Yo-Yo Teacher" on page 42? Use details from the article to support your answer.

13 Compare and contrast how to do the tricks Sleeper and Walk the Dog. Describe **one** way the tricks are similar and **one** way they are different. Use details from the article to support your answer.

14 Even though a yo-yo is simple, yo-yoing can be challenging. Describe the **two** main factors that make yo-yoing challenging. Use details from the article to support your answer.

Planning Space

You can write notes, make a list, or draw a chart to help plan your answer.

15 The article states that yo-yo masters are chosen "for their skill with the yo-yo and for their hard work to promote the yo-yo in their communities." Explain how Dave meets both these measures. Use details from the article to support your answer.

Planning Space

You can write notes, make a list, or draw a chart to help plan your answer.

_____

_____

_____

_____

_____

_____

_____

_____

_____

_____

_____

_____

_____

Directions: Read the passage. Then answer the questions that follow it.

The Dishonest Merchant
A Romanian Legend

Retold by David Roper

1   Once upon a time, a prince known for his intolerance of dishonesty ruled in Romania. During his reign, a greedy merchant from another country traveled through the land.

2   During one journey, the merchant lost a bag containing one thousand Romanian coins called *lei*. Each time the merchant came to a crossroads, he told everyone that he would give one hundred lei to anyone who found the money.

3   Not long afterward, a peasant found the bag. He was an honest man, and he hastened to find the merchant.

4   "I found this bag behind the fish market at the crossroads near my home," the peasant said to the merchant.

5   The merchant trusted no one, so he went aside to count the money. To his surprise, all one thousand coins were still in the bag. He was happy to have his money back, but he was also saddened by the thought of giving some of it away. He wondered how he could get out of his promise and still appear to be fair.

6   At last he went back to the peasant. "I thank you for returning my money," he said. "I notice that you have already taken your reward, for there were only nine hundred coins in the bag."

7   The peasant protested. "But I did not even open the bag before I gave it to you!"

8   The merchant ignored the peasant's words. "I hope you enjoy your reward," he said. "Thank you again and good-bye." He quickly departed.

9   The peasant was upset— not just because he had received no reward but because he had been accused of taking money without permission. He hurried to the palace and requested to see the prince. He told his sad story, and the prince promised that he would uncover the truth.

10   The prince sent word for the merchant and the peasant to appear before him on a certain day. He told the merchant to bring the bag of money.

11   When the day arrived, the merchant told his side of the story and the peasant told his. As the prince listened, it became obvious to him that the peasant was telling the truth.

12   When they had finished, the prince said to the merchant, "You lost a bag with one thousand coins. Is that correct?"

13   "Yes," said the merchant.

14 The prince took the money bag, which now held only nine hundred lei. "And when you were handed this bag, it contained only nine hundred coins?"

15 "That is true," said the merchant, trying to look sincere.

16 "I am sure that you are telling the truth," said the prince, "for nothing is punished so severely in this court as dishonesty. However, these facts present me with a problem."

17 The prince held up the bag for all to see. It was an ordinary leather bag, like thousands of others. He asked the merchant, "If your bag contained one thousand coins and this bag has only nine hundred, then how do you know this is your bag?"

18 The merchant had trouble speaking. "I ... I," he stammered. Then he was silent.

19 The prince continued. "It is obvious that this is not your bag. My verdict therefore is that you should continue to inquire at the crossroads until you find your bag with one thousand lei. I wish you well in your quest."

20 The prince turned to the peasant. "And I decree that you take care of this bag of nine hundred coins until the rightful owner comes forth. If we do not find the owner within three months, then the money will be yours as a reward for your honesty."

21 There was nothing more to say, since there could be no appeal regarding the prince's verdict. The dishonest merchant and the honest peasant left the prince's chamber, the first very sad and the other very happy.

22 This was how dishonesty was treated in the days of the prince.

Directions: Answer the following questions. If you need more space to write an answer, write your answer on your own paper.

1 What main quality of the merchant causes him to choose not to give the reward?

A   jealousy

B   impatience

C   greed

D   laziness

2 Read this sentence from the story.

"The peasant was upset—not just because he had received no reward but because he had been accused of taking money without permission."

This sentence is mainly included to show that the peasant—

A   has pride.

B   is determined.

C   has a short temper.

D   trusts people too easily.

3 The outcome for the merchant offers readers a lesson about—

A   being prepared.

B   keeping your promises.

C   working hard.

D   asking others for help.

4 Which sentence best supports the message of the story?

A "I found this bag behind the fish market at the crossroads near my home," the peasant said to the merchant.

B The peasant was upset—not just because he had received no reward but because he had been accused of taking money without permission.

C "I am sure that you are telling the truth," said the prince, "for nothing is punished so severely in this court as dishonesty."

D The dishonest merchant and the honest peasant left the prince's chamber, the first very sad and the other very happy.

5 Based on the story, the reader can tell that the prince is—

A angry.

B clever.

C lazy.

D proud.

6 Which sentence from the story best supports the idea that the prince is clever?

A He told his sad story, and the prince promised that he would uncover the truth.

B The prince sent word for the merchant and the peasant to appear before him on a certain day.

C When they had finished, the prince said to the merchant, "You lost a bag with one thousand coins."

D He asked the merchant, "If your bag contained one thousand coins and this bag has only nine hundred, then how do you know this is your bag?"

7 The peasant most likely went to the prince because he wanted to—

   A receive more money as a reward.

   B see that the merchant was punished.

   C prove that he did not take the money.

   D show that he was not afraid of the merchant.

8 In the end, the peasant got all the money because he—

   A found the bag on the road.

   B was honest.

   C traveled to another country.

   D told others about the missing money.

9 In paragraph 16, the prince says that he is sure the merchant is telling the truth. Does the prince mean what he says? Use at least **two** details from the story to support your answer.

10 Read this sentence from paragraph 17.

"It was an ordinary leather bag, like thousands of others."

Why is this detail important to the plot of the story? Use details from the story to support your answer.

11 How does the merchant feel when the prince asks him how he can know it is his bag? Use at least **two** specific details from the story to support your answer.

12 The prince says that the peasant can keep all the coins if the rightful owner does not come forward. How can you tell that the rightful owner will not come forward? Use details from the story to support your answer.

13 The merchant does not give the reward because he does not want to lose one hundred coins. How does the ending of the story make this decision seem amusing? Use details from the story to support your answer.

14 If the same events happened again, which main character do you think would be most likely to act differently? Use details from the story to explain why you chose either the peasant or the merchant.

15 The outcome of the story is described in paragraphs 19 to 21. How do the merchant's and the peasant's actions at the beginning lead to the final outcome? Explain whether the outcome is fair for the peasant and the merchant. Use information from the story to support your answer.

Planning Space

You can complete the charts below to help plan your answer.

Merchant's Actions

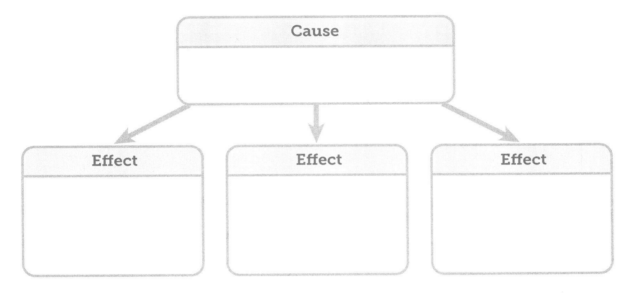

Peasant's Actions

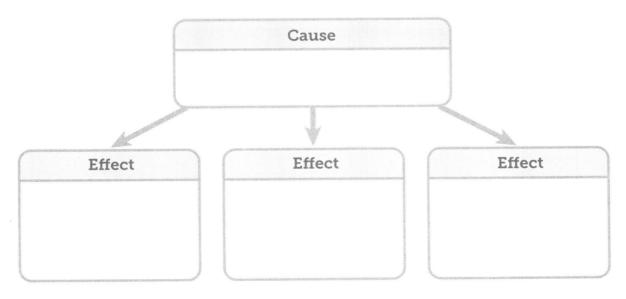

Directions: Read the passage. Then answer the questions that follow it.

Harry Truman, Lost and Found

By Janice Jump

1   In 1892, children seldom wore glasses, but eight-year-old Harry S. Truman was different. He was probably the only one in his class to have spectacles.

2   Harry's mother, Martha, had noticed something odd about his eyesight. Harry was a very early reader and spent much time reading the large-print family Bible. But he couldn't make out smaller print or see anything from a distance.

3   At a Fourth of July celebration, everyone watched the exploding fireworks except Harry. He jumped when the rockets blasted but was unable to see them.

4   Martha Ellen Truman realized her son needed help. She hitched up her horses and took Harry to an eye specialist. The doctor diagnosed Harry's condition as "flat eyeballs" and fitted him with thick lenses. He warned Harry to be careful and told him not to get involved in any rough play.

5   Harry's spectacles opened a new world for him.

6   "When I first put the glasses on I saw things and saw print I'd never seen before," he later said.

7   Harry loved history. His favorite books were *Great Men and Famous Women*, a four-volume set edited by Charles Francis Horne, a gift from his mother on his twelfth birthday.

8   Harry was teased and called "sissy" because he spent so much time reading. His mother insisted that fighting was for babies, so Harry resisted the temptation and went to the library instead.

9 "I was too busy reading books to be bad," Truman later said. "I'd read all three thousand books in the library by the time I was fourteen years old."

10 Reading wasn't Harry's only interest. He also wanted to play baseball. But Harry's mother didn't want him to play sports. She was afraid he might break his expensive glasses. Harry figured out a way to make it happen. When a neighborhood baseball game started, he volunteered to be the umpire, knowing his glasses would be safely hidden under his umpire mask.

11 Throughout his life, Harry was always concerned about his glasses. Lucky for him, good fortune followed him and his glasses. On three dangerous occasions at different times in his life, Harry Truman and his glasses escaped safe and sound.

Soldier Truman

12 In 1917 the United States entered World War I. At the age of thirty-three, Harry became a lieutenant in the U.S. Army. He took along three extra pairs of glasses when he left for France.

13 During maneuvers against the German forces, his horse, Dobbin, rode too close to a low-hanging branch. Harry's glasses were brushed off. He glanced down the path, but they had vanished. There was no time to fetch his extra pair from the supply wagon. Harry was frantic. He was in the middle of a battle, and he was as blind as a bat.

14 Then he spied something shining on his horse's rump. It was his glasses!

Senator Truman

15 In 1935 Harry S. Truman became a U.S. senator. During his six-year term, he and his family traveled to their home in Independence, Missouri, to spend summer vacations.

16 On one trip, the family was involved in an automobile accident. Senator Truman was wearing his glasses, but he couldn't see the stop sign.

17 It was blocked by a parked car. He drove through the intersection, and another car crashed into them.

18 The car suffered extensive damage, but Senator Truman and his wife, Bess, suffered only minor injuries. His daughter, Margaret, was safe in the back seat.

19 The senator's glasses were found on the floor—without a scratch! He had flung them over his shoulder in a desperate attempt to save them.

President Truman

20 On April 12, 1945, Harry S. Truman became the thirty-third President of the United States. After being elected to a second term, President Truman took his family on a vacation to Key West, Florida.

21 President Truman and his daughter went to the beach. Harry jumped into the water and coaxed her to follow, but Margaret sat on the seawall and watched.

22 Suddenly a large wave knocked Truman over, and under he went. The Secret Service men came to the rescue.

23 President Truman was fine, but his glasses were gone!

24 Truman had extra pairs in his room, but the Secret Service insisted upon looking for them. Unfortunately, they couldn't find the President's glasses.

25 Later, Truman sat on the seawall and relaxed. He noticed a patch of light on the sandy beach. Truman summoned the Secret Service men, and they investigated. It was his glasses. They had been washed up by the tide.

In almost every picture of Harry S. Truman you'll notice he's wearing glasses. There is a rare exception—Truman's face on the photograph used on his army AEF (American Expeditionary Forces) Identity Card when he was a captain.

The photograph shows Truman from the waist up. One can only guess that Truman was holding his glasses.

Directions: Answer the following questions. If you need more space to write an answer, write your answer on your own paper.

1 Which sentence from the article best summarizes the main idea?

A "In 1892, children seldom wore glasses, but eight-year-old Harry S. Truman was different."

B "The doctor diagnosed Harry's condition as 'flat eyeballs' and fitted him with thick lenses."

C "His mother insisted that fighting was for babies, so Harry resisted the temptation and went to the library instead."

D "On three dangerous occasions at different times in his life, Harry Truman and his glasses escaped safe and sound."

2 In paragraph 9, Truman is quoted saying, "I'd read all three thousand books in the library by the time I was fourteen years old." Why is this quote important in the article?

A It emphasizes his love for books.

B It suggests that he had few friends.

C It explains how he learned about history.

D It indicates why he was successful in his life.

3 Read these sentences from the end of the article.

"The photograph shows Truman from the waist up. One can only guess that Truman was holding his glasses."

What is the author implying in these sentences?

A Truman's glasses were so important to him that he was probably not actually without them.

B Truman would have preferred not to wear glasses, but recognized that he needed them.

C Truman was lucky often, but probably lost his glasses at least once.

D Truman was always prepared, so he often had a spare pair of glasses with him.

4 On page 69, under the picture of Harry Truman without his glasses, the authors writes, "One can only guess that Truman was holding his glasses." Which sentence from the article best supports this idea?

   A He was probably the only one in his class to have spectacles.

   B Harry's spectacles opened a new world for him.

   C Throughout his life, Harry was always concerned about his glasses.

   D Lucky for him, good fortune followed him and his glasses.

5 What event caused Martha Ellen Truman to seek out an eye specialist to help Harry?

   A Harry could not see a stop sign when driving his car.

   B Harry could not see fireworks on the Fourth of July.

   C Harry could not see the letters in a large-print Bible.

   D Harry could not see the enemy forces during the war.

6 The section of the article titled "Senator Truman" is mainly about—

   A a car accident.

   B a family vacation.

   C Truman's election.

   D Truman's hometown.

7 Read these two pairs of sentences from the article.

> *The doctor diagnosed Harry's condition as 'flat eyeballs' and fitted him with thick lenses. He warned Harry to be careful and told him not to get involved in any rough play.*
>
> *But Harry's mother didn't want him to play sports. She was afraid he might break his expensive glasses.*

Which of these describes the connection between the two pairs of sentences?

A Both explain how Harry's first pair of glasses looked.

B Both describe the effects of Harry's glasses on his eyesight.

C Both suggest causes of Harry's lifelong worry about his glasses.

D Both hint that Harry's glasses helped to better his reading skills.

8 Which of these is the best summary of the article?

A Harry Truman started wearing glasses at the age of eight. He was always very careful with his glasses. However, he lost them many times. Most pictures of Harry show him wearing glasses.

B Harry Truman began wearing glasses as a child and wore them for his whole life. He was always careful with his glasses. However, he still lost them several times. Luckily, he always found them again.

C Harry Truman began wearing glasses at the age of eight. He liked that his glasses helped him see well. However, he feared that his glasses would get broken if he played sports. For this reason, he wore a mask when he played baseball.

D Harry Truman could not see well as a child. His mother took him to get glasses when he was eight years old. The glasses helped him see well. He continued wearing glasses for the rest of his life. He is wearing glasses in almost every picture of him.

9 Harry needed glasses as a boy because of his poor eyesight. How does the author emphasize how poor Harry's eyesight was? Use at least **two** specific examples from the article to support your answer.

10 Read the anecdote about Harry playing baseball in paragraph 10. What does the anecdote reveal about Harry's character? Use details from the article to support your answer.

11 In paragraph 5, the author states that Harry's spectacles "opened a new world for him." Explain what this "new world" was and why it was important to Harry. Use details from the article to support your answer.

12 How does Harry's childhood help explain how much his glasses meant to him later in life? Use details from the article to support your answer.

13 Summarize the lucky event described in the section "Soldier Truman."
Why was it so important for Harry to get his glasses back? Use details
from the article to support your answer.

14 The title of the article is "Harry Truman, Lost and Found." Explain how this
title summarizes the main idea of the article. Use details from the article to
support your answer.

15 The article describes three "dangerous occasions" where Harry S. Truman was lucky not to lose his glasses. Explain why each event was lucky. Which event do you feel involved the most luck? Which event would have been most dangerous if he had lost his glasses? Use information from the article to support your answer.

Planning Space

You can complete the chart below to help plan your answer.

	Why was the event lucky?	How lucky was the event?	How would losing glasses be dangerous?
Event in "Soldier Truman"			
Event in "Senator Truman"			
Event in "President Truman"			

_____

_____

_____

_____

_____

_____

_____

_____

_____

_____

_____

_____

Part B:

Craft and Structure

Literary, Informational, and Paired Passages with Multiple Choice, Short Response, Extended Response, and Essay Questions

Reading Standards

R.4.4   Determine the meaning of general academic and domain-specific words or phrases in a text relevant to a grade 4 topic or subject area. Determine the meaning of words and phrases as they are used in a text, including those that allude to significant characters found in mythology (e.g., Herculean).

⬤ **Informational**   ⬤ **Literary**

R.4.5   Describe the overall structure (e.g., chronology, comparison, cause/effect, problem/solution) of events, ideas, concepts, or information in a text or part of a text. Explain major differences between poems, drama, and prose, and refer to the structural elements of poems (e.g., verse, rhythm, meter) and drama (e.g., casts of characters, settings, descriptions, dialogue, stage directions) when writing or speaking about a text.

⬤ **Informational**   ⬤ **Literary**

R.4.6   Compare and contrast a firsthand and secondhand account of the same event or topic; describe the differences in focus and the information provided. Compare and contrast the point of view from which different stories are narrated, including the difference between first- and third-person narrations.

⬤ **Informational**   ⬤ **Literary**

Instruction

Directions: Read the passage. The guides in the blue bar will help you focus on some of the important details. Then answer the questions that follow. These questions will also have guides to help you find the correct answers.

Career Cat

By Irene A. Flores
Art by Phoenix Chan

Look at the title. Look at the illustrations. What do you think this passage will be about?

1   "I'm sorry," Bonnie's best friend Cleo meowed one morning. Bonnie had just wandered into the library from her home in the alley. "You're going to have to get a job if you want to keep the canned tuna coming."

2   First, Bonnie tried looking at Cleo with her big, pleading Siamese-blue eyes. That usually got her a couple pieces of kitty-kibble, at the very least. But what Bonnie really liked best was tuna.

3　"Right now all I can afford is dry food," her friend insisted.

4　Bonnie let her tail droop in defeat and sat down hard on her bottom. She looked up at Cleo, the library's resident black cat, and asked how she had gotten *her* job.

5　"It wasn't easy, let me tell you." Cleo sat like a queen atop her pile of books, her black tail twitching back and forth. "You have to be firm and you have to meow at the humans just right."

6　Bonnie thought she could do that. Library work didn't sound too hard. Bonnie could stare at humans evilly until they picked up a book. She could dust the shelves with her tail, even if it was a bit petite. Never mind that her stare was awkward and clueless instead of scary like Cleo's.

What is the best way for cats to afford their own food?

7　"Fine," Cleo said. "I guess I could take you on as an assistant."

8　With a mighty leap, Bonnie tried to climb onto a bookshelf. But for such a young kitten, Bonnie possessed an enormous bottom. To her horror, it pulled her back down with an awful crash.

9　"Try again," Cleo hissed in annoyance.

10　And Bonnie did try. Again and again and again.

11　"Seems like you're going to have to look for another job."

12 Bonnie flattened her ears in embarrassment and bolted out of the library. But it would be nice to work close to home, she thought. Maybe she could still find something nearby.

Why doesn't Bonnie's first job work out with Cleo?

13 She crossed the park to Suds-R-Us, the Laundromat on the other side, and asked for a job.

14 "Well," said the human behind the counter. "I guess I could use the help. You can start by folding clothes."

15 Being a fussy sort of kitten, Bonnie was well suited to tasks like folding up clothing. She did a beautiful job of it—without a single wrinkle! She filled many plastic bags with freshly folded laundry.

16 At the end of the day she mewed proudly for her pay.

17 "I can't deliver these!" shrieked her boss after one look at the clothes. "They're covered in WHITE FUR! And most of them are black!"

18   Bonnie shot out the door quicker than you could say "meow" and without even a penny. According to the human, her pay would go toward washing and drying those clothes all over again.

Why doesn't Bonnie get paid for her job at the laundromat?

19   Bonnie dragged herself back to the sidewalk and sat there, sighing miserably. Maybe the guy who ran the corner store would charge a can of tuna to Cleo's tab…

20   As she turned toward the store, she saw a sign she had never seen before. It spelled M-A-S-S-A-G-E-S and had a human paw print beneath it. Right there, through the window, was something Bonnie could do!

21   "I don't know," said the massage therapist while he examined his patient's shoulders. "Why don't you show me your technique?"

22   Off went Bonnie, kneading the carpet with all the strength in her little paws! Every cat is an expert in this area, but Bonnie was a champion kneader. She had heard humans shout, "I can feel that through the blanket!"

23   "You're hired!" said her new boss. "That looks fantastic!"

24   Bonnie hadn't even finished with her first client when she was thrown out on her fluffy, white behind.

25   "Ow! Ow!" the patient screamed. "She nearly scratched my skin off!"

26   Nobody had told her she was supposed to keep her claws covered.

27 Bonnie plodded back over to the park and sat beneath a tree, feeling sorry for herself. If only she could be a sleek and smart career cat like Cleo. Then she could pay for tuna and kitty treats. She could even afford a rubber mouse for herself! She was a no-good failure of a kitten.

28 "I am a no-good failure of a man!" A man in a suit slumped beside Bonnie under the tree. His clothes were wrinkled and he had bags under his eyes the size of suitcases.

29 "I can't keep being late to work or I'll be fired!"

What do Bonnie and the man who is always late have in common?

30 Suddenly, Bonnie turned her big Siamese-blue eyes to him.

31 Oh, if there was one thing she was really great at…

• • •

32 Every day at seven in the morning, Bonnie wakes up and carefully washes her paws and face. She sets off in a busy trot, slips into her client's apartment building, and takes the elevator to the sixth floor. She enters apartment 603 through a kitty door.

33 Once inside, in the manner of cats all over the world, she sits on the side of his face until he wakes up. She's so good at waking up her human that sometimes all it takes is a mournful stare and whiny mew, and her boss will jump right out of bed. He'll never be late for work again!

34 Each day, she buys a shiny can of tuna with a cheerful fish on the label. Every once in a while, if she has a bit of time, she will chirp a greeting to Cleo on her bookshelf. But she is a professional now and can lose no time chatting.

1 Which of the following statements best shows one of Bonnie's bosses being frustrated with her?

A "I can't deliver these!"

B "I guess I could use the help."

C "You're going to have to get a job if you want to keep the canned tuna coming."

D "I can't keep being late to work or I'll be fired!"

This is a **Point of View** question. In this section, the **point of view** shifts from Bonnie to one of Bonnie's bosses.

---

2 Read the following quote from the story.

"I am a no-good failure of a man!"

Why does the man in the park say this?

A He feels disappointed in himself for not being on time to his job.

B He has been fired from his job and has nowhere to go.

C The woman he truly loved has left him.

D The job he wanted has been taken by someone else.

This is a **Vocabulary in Context** question. What is a failure? How does the man probably feel when he makes this statement?

---

3 Read the following sentence from the story.

"Every day at seven in the morning, Bonnie wakes up and carefully washes her paws and face."

What feeling is Bonnie showing here?

A sadness

B self-pity

C anger

D pride

This is a **Point of View** question. This part of the passage is told from the **point of view** of an outside narrator. Do you think they know how Bonnie is feeling?

4 If this story had been written from the point of view of the man for whom Bonnie begins working, what might have been different about it?

A We would learn more about why Cleo told Bonnie that Bonnie had to get a job.

B We would learn what the woman at the Laundromat did after Bonnie left.

C We would learn how much he appreciates Bonnie for waking him up every morning.

D We would learn what his boss said about him when he wasn't around at work.

> This is a **Point of View** question. What would the man know or not know about Bonnie and her work habits?

5 Read the following sentence from the story, in which Cleo is giving Bonnie instructions.

> *"'You have to be firm and you have to meow at the humans just right.'"*

Which word best describes what Cleo is teaching Bonnie to be?

A persuasive

B boring

C nice

D sad

> This is a **Vocabulary in Context** question. Which word is similar to **firm**?

6 Read the following sentence from the story.

> *"Bonnie shot out the door quicker than you could say 'meow' and without even a penny."*

Why does Bonnie do this?

A She is late for an appointment.

B She feels badly about what the woman told her.

C She cannot wait to go tell Cleo about her day.

D She has to go wake up the man for work.

This is a **Point of View** question. How is Bonnie feeling at this point in the story?

---

7 Read the following sentence from the story.

> *"First, Bonnie tried looking at Cleo with her big, pleading Siamese-blue eyes."*

Which word is closest in meaning to "pleading"?

A laughing

B crying

C begging

D sleeping

This is a **Vocabulary in Context** question. What does it mean when you plead for something?

8 Read this sentence from the story.

> *"I can't deliver these!" shrieked her boss after one look at the clothes. "They're covered in WHITE FUR! And most of them are black!"*

Describe the relationship between these three sentences. Use details from the sentences to support your answer.

This is a **Structure** question. This story is told in sentences that are connected. How are these three sentences connected?

9 When Bonnie "flattened her ears in embarrassment," what made her do this? Use details from the story to support your answer.

This is a **Point of View** question. How is Bonnie feeling at this point in the story?

10 What is the problem described in the first paragraph? How is this problem solved? Use details from the story to support your answer.

This is a **Structure** question. How does the story change from beginning to end? Is the problem solved?

11 How does Bonnie's being a "fussy cat" relate to her ability to fold clothing? Use details from the story to support your answer.

This is a **Vocabulary in Context** question. When someone acts fussy, how are they behaving?

12   Why is this story titled "Career Cat"? Use details from the story to support your answer.

This is a **Point of View** question. By naming Career Cat as the title, the author wants you to know right away whose point of view is telling this story.

13   How does Bonnie's last job make her feel? Use details from the story to support your answer.

This is a **Point of View** question. Does Bonnie feel better or worse at her last job?

14 This story is told from a third-person point of view. Think about how the story would be different if it was told from a first-person point of view. Pick two characters and tell how the story would be different if it were told from their point of view.

Planning Space

You can write notes, make a list, or draw a chart to help plan your answer.

This is a **Point of View** question. In this instance, first-person point of view would be if Bonnie was telling the story directly.

_____

_____

_____

_____

_____

_____

_____

_____

_____

_____

_____

_____

15 Use the graphic organizer to explain what happened with three different jobs that Bonnie had in the story.

This is a **Point of View** question. In this instance, first-person point of view would be if Bonnie was telling the story directly.

Planning Space

You can complete the chart below to help plan your answer.

Job	What Happened?

_____

_____

_____

_____

_____

_____

_____

_____

_____

_____

_____

_____

_____

Directions: Read the passage. The guides in the blue bar will help you focus on some of the important details. Then answer the questions that follow. These questions will also have guides to help you find the correct answers.

Kids on the High Seas

By Dave and Jaja Martin

Look at the title. Look at the illustration. What do you think this passage will be about?

1   Chris, Holly, and Teiga live on a sailboat. With their mom and dad, they sail all over the world. You can't have a much better view of the ocean than that. It's kind of like having the ocean for your backyard.

2   One summer they sail from the United States all the way across the ocean to a country called Iceland. The voyage lasts 23 days. That's a long time to spend on a small boat at sea, but everything the children need is on board. They have food, water, clothes, and toys. They don't have a television, but they have fun coloring, playing with Legos, reading books, and listening to music.

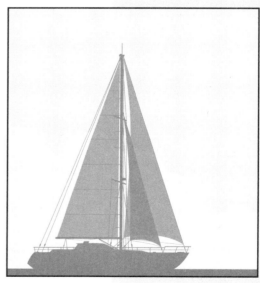

3   Sometimes it storms. When the boat dances wildly in the big waves, simple tasks such as putting on clothes, eating, brushing your teeth, or going to the bathroom become hard work. The bathroom on the boat, called the "head," has handles mounted on the walls for hanging on to.

How does life on the sailboat change during bad weather?

4   During mealtimes in a storm, Chris, Holly, and Teiga wedge themselves onto a bunk. That's a bed built into a wall. A chair would just slide around. Mom hands them bowls of food and they eat slowly. When they are finished, Mom takes the bowls away and

hands them cups of juice. It's too bumpy to hold a bowl and a cup at the same time. The best part of a storm is when it's over. During bad weather, Dad keeps watch outside up on deck and the children have to stay inside the cabin. When the sea smooths again, they are allowed to go on deck and play.

5   At first glance, the middle of the ocean seems empty. All you see are water and sky. But if you look hard, you'll notice a lot. Even far away from land, birds skim the water searching for food. Dolphins swim in crisscross paths under the front of the boat, called the bow. If you are lucky, you might glimpse a huge whale gliding across the water's surface. And sooner or later, you spot land.

What sort of animals live in the open ocean?

6   On the twenty-third day at sea, the children spy the barren hills of Iceland. As the boat sails nearer to land, they begin to see lighthouses and buoys, then buses, cars, and people walking!

7   As soon as the boat is tied up in the harbor, the family ventures into the heart of Reykjavik, Iceland's capital city. After the long ocean voyage, the noise and commotion of the busy streets are bewildering. Everyone on land seems in such a hurry! The children sit in a park and look at the green grass and trees. Flowers blossom in vivid colors. After seeing only a blue ocean and a blue sky for many weeks, all these colors seem like rare treasures. But what did the children miss most while they were at sea? Ice cream!

What is exciting about Reykjavik, Iceland?

8   Exploring Iceland will be fun, but Chris, Holly, and Teiga can't wait to set sail again. Exploring the ocean is their family's favorite thing to do.

1 Read the following sentence from the passage.

"After the long ocean voyage, the noise and commotion of the busy streets are bewildering."

Which word below is closest in meaning to "bewildering"?

A humorous

B confusing

C boring

D good

This is a **Vocabulary in Context** question. When you are bewildered by something, how do you think you will feel?

---

2 Read the following sentence from the story.

"Dolphins swim in crisscross paths under the front of the boat, called the bow."

Which is the best description of what it would mean for the dolphins to swim in "crisscross paths?"

A square paths

B paths behind the boat

C disappearing paths

D back and forth paths

This is a **Vocabulary in Context** question. Crisscross makes a special type of pattern. What would it most likely look like when something crosses in front of something else?

3 Which paragraph best explains the main event or idea of this informational passage?

A paragraph 2

B paragraph 6

C paragraph 1

D paragraph 5

This is a **Chronology** question. In this passage, you need to go back and look for the correct day and paragraph in which a main event takes place.

4 Read the following sentence from the passage.

"When the boat dances wildly in the big waves, simple tasks such as putting on clothes, eating, brushing your teeth, or going to the bathroom become hard work."

Which word below is closest in meaning to "wildly"?

A violently

B lazily

C calmly

D slowly

This is a **Vocabulary in Context** question. When something is acting wild, how is it acting?

5 Read the following sentence from the passage.

"Exploring the ocean is their family's favorite thing to do."

Which word is the closest in meaning to "exploring"?

A coughing

B investigating

C leaving

D asking

This is a **Vocabulary in Context** question. When you explore, what are you doing?

---

6 Read the following sentence from the passage.

"During mealtimes in a storm, Chris, Holly, and Teiga wedge themselves onto a bunk."

Why do the kids have to "wedge" themselves onto a bunk?

A They have to go to bed right after they finish eating.

B They have to because that is what their parents have made them do.

C They will be punished if they do not.

D They will slide around too much if they sat in a chair.

This is a **Cause/Effect** question. Wedge is the vocabulary word, but there is a reason why the kids must do this activity.

---

7 What is the author's purpose in terms of the structure and form of this passage?

A to explain about life on the sea

B to try to convince people to live on the sea

C to tell why living on the sea is not good

D to explain facts about dolphins

This is a **Structure** question. You are trying to find out how the author uses structure and form to illustrate important ideas. Which idea is most likely to happen?

8 Read the following sentence from the passage.

> *"At first glance, the middle of the ocean seems empty."*

How does the rest of the paragraph give additional information on what is described in this sentence? Use details from the passage to support your answer.

This is a **Structure** question. Read the rest of this paragraph to see how it builds upon the given sentence.

9 Read the following sentence from the passage.

> *"Everyone on land seems in such a hurry!"*

Why might the people on land be in a hurry? Use details from the passage to support your answer.

This is a **Vocabulary in Context** question. "In a hurry" means you are rushing around to get somewhere quickly.

10 The passage says that "everything the children need is on board." Explain how this is true, using details from the text.

This is a **Vocabulary in Context** question. "On board" means that all of their belongings are on the boat.

11 The passage says that living on a sailboat is "kind of like having the ocean for your backyard." How is this supported by the passage? Use details from the passage to support your answer.

This is a **Compare and Contrast** question. The author is saying that these people have water in their backyard, as opposed to most people, who live on land.

12 What does the author's metaphor (non-literal language) that the boat dances "wildly in the big waves" tell us about the boat? How is this supported by the rest of the paragraph?

This is a **Vocabulary in Context** question. What is the boat doing? How is it affecting the rest of the people on the boat?

13 Read the following sentence from the passage.

"Exploring the ocean is their family's favorite thing to do."

How is this idea supported by the rest of the passage?

This is a **Structure** question. Read the rest of the sentences in this paragraph to see how it builds upon the previous sections.

14 This passage is written in secondhand point of view. Choose one person from the passage. What might be different if this was told in firsthand point of view of one of the people in the passage?

Planning Space

You can write notes, make a list, or draw a chart to help plan your answer.

This is a **Point of View** question. A secondhand person may not be on the boat with this family. How would their experiences be different? How would this be expressed in the passage?

_____

_____

_____

_____

_____

_____

_____

_____

_____

_____

_____

_____

_____

15 Fill out the following chart about different locations in the passage. What language is used to describe these particular locations? What does this language tell us about the locations?

This is a **Vocabulary in Context** question. You need to look for the type of language the author uses to describe places and what this language shows about each location.

Planning Space

You can complete the chart below to help plan your answer.

Location	Language Used to Describe the Location	What the Language Tells Us About the Location
Boat		
Ocean		
Iceland		

_____

_____

_____

_____

_____

_____

_____

_____

_____

_____

_____

_____

_____

_____

Independent Practice

Directions: Read the play. Then answer the questions that follow it.

The Wise Men of Gotham

Adapted from a Play by Augusta Stevenson

SCENE I

TIME: one morning long ago
PLACE: the highroad to Gotham

1   *[Enter* HODGE, PODGE, NODGE, *and* SCRODGE; *each carries an ax and each chuckles to himself.]*

2   HODGE: Well, the last tree is down!

3   PODGE: Down and across the road!

4   NODGE: Not a horse can get through them!

5   SCRODGE: How angry it will make the king! He would hang us if he knew we cut the trees and let them fall across the road.

6   PODGE: He will not know. Not a Gotham man would tell him!

7   HODGE: They have not forgotten what havoc his last visit brought upon them.

8   PODGE: Everything he saw and liked, he took.

9   NODGE: And would not pay for it!

10   PODGE *(looking off)*: He is coming now! He is on the hill!

11   SCRODGE: He has his soldiers with him!

12   NODGE: He must not see us! Come!

13   *[They run off. Enter the* KING *and* SOLDIERS.]*

14   KING: Look how the road from here is filled with trees!

15   SOLDIER: Just as it was back there!

16   KING: I know! It was done to keep me out of Gotham! I know! *(He stamps his feet.)* Here, you!

17   SOLDIER *(saluting)*: Yes, your Majesty.

18   KING: Get to Gotham, if you have to crawl. Tell these men of Gotham I shall come again.

19   SOLDIER: Yes, your Majesty.

20   KING: And when I do—and when I do—[*He stops.*]

21   SOLDIER: Yes, your Majesty?

22   KING: And when I do, I'll have their noses! I'll have the Gotham nose of every Gotham man cut off his Gotham face! Go, now, and tell them that!

23   SOLDIER *(saluting)*: Yes, your Majesty.

24   [*He goes.*]

25   KING: We will now return the way we came. *(He shakes his finger toward Gotham.)* I'll have your noses, that I will!

26   [*He goes with his soldiers.*]

SCENE II

TIME: one month later
PLACE: a field near Gotham

27   [*The* OLD MEN, *the* YOUNG MEN, *and the* CHILDREN *are in the field.*]

28   AN OLD MAN: Well, the king's men have taken all the trees away.

29   A YOUNG MAN: A good month's work it made them, too!

30 ANOTHER OLD MAN: And now the king will come again!

31 *[Enter* HODGE, PODGE, NODGE, *and* SCRODGE.*]*

32 SCRODGE: The king is coming!

33 CHILDREN: Oh dear! We'll lose our noses!

34 HODGE: Now get you back to Gotham, children! You will not lose your noses.

35 PODGE: Quick, now—before the king comes!

36 *[The children go, holding their noses.]*

37 NODGE: Now, Gotham men, do you all know what to do?

38 OLD MEN: Aye! Aye!

39 YOUNG MEN: Aye! Aye!

40 *[All the men begin to work.]*

41 PODGE: I think this will save our noses.

42 *[Enter the* KING *and the* SOLDIERS.*]*

43 KING: Is there a tree left on the road?

44 SOLDIER: We took them all away, Sire.

45 KING: Then go and get our horses. We will ride into this Gotham town. *(The soldier salutes and goes.)* Where do you roll these stones, old men?

46 AN OLD MAN: Uphill to help the sun rise.

47 KING: What! To help the sun rise?

48 OLD MAN: Yes, your Majesty.

49 KING: Don't you know that the sun will rise without help?

50   OLD MAN: Will it? Well, well! Who would have thought of that!

51   KING: You foolish fellows! Well, go on and roll your stones. Now tell me why you grunt, young men?

52   A YOUNG MAN: Oh, we do the grunting while our fathers do the work.

53   KING: Ha, ha! Well, go on and grunt. Now what are you men doing?

54   HODGE: There is a cuckoo here, your Majesty. We are building a wall around it, Sire.

55   KING: Why build a wall around it?

56   NODGE: To keep it from flying away.

57   KING: Ha, ha! Don't you know that the bird can fly over the wall?

58   HODGE: Well, well! Who would have thought of that! How very wise you are, Sire!

59 KING: You foolish fellows! Well, go on and build your wall. *(Enter SCRODGE, carrying a door on his back.)* Where are you going with that door?

60 SCRODGE: I am going on a journey, Sire.

61 KING: Why do you carry a door?

62 SCRODGE: I left my money at home, Sire.

63 KING: Why didn't you leave the door at home?

64 SCRODGE: I was afraid of thieves. If I have the door with me, they can't break it open to get in.

65 KING: You foolish fellow! Why didn't you leave your door at home and carry your money?

66 SCRODGE: Well, well! Who would have thought of that! How very wise you are, Sire!

67 KING: Ha, ha, ha! Well, go on and carry your door. *(To Soldiers.)* These Gotham men are foolish. Does it not seem so to you?

68 SOLDIERS: Aye, Sire!

69 KING: I'll let them keep their noses. They knew no better than to cut down the trees. Come, we will go away and leave them.

70 *[The KING and SOLDIERS go.]*

71 GOTHAM MEN: Ha, ha, ha!

Directions: Answer the following questions. If you need more space to write an answer, write your answer on your own paper.

1 Read this line from Scene I.

> *"HODGE: They have not forgotten what havoc his last visit brought upon them."*

What does the word *havoc* mean?

A excitement

B joy

C disorder

D sadness

2 In the first scene, what is the main reason the king is angry about the fallen trees?

A He fears he will have to pay to fix the road.

B He believes the men are wasting important timber.

C He thinks the men are trying to keep him away.

D He worries that the trees may harm his horses.

3 Read this sentence from the play:

> *A YOUNG MAN: A good month's work it made them, too!*

What does this sentence from the play mean?

A they earned a month's wages

B it was not hard work

C it was hard work that took a long time to do

D the work was very good

4 Read line 16.

> *KING: I know! It was done to keep me out of Gotham! I know!*
>
> *(He stamps his feet.) Here, you!*

The words in parentheses emphasize the king's—

A anger

B excitement

C nervousness

D power

5 Read lines 35 and 36.

> *PODGE: Quick, now—before the king comes!*
>
> *[The children go, holding their noses.]*

The words in the brackets show that the children—

A smell something bad

B are afraid of the king

C are unfriendly to the men

D feel like they are getting sick

6 Read lines 37 through 39.

> *NODGE: Now, Gotham men, do you all know what to do?*
>
> *OLD MEN: Aye! Aye!*
>
> *YOUNG MEN: Aye! Aye!*

The dialogue in these lines shows that the men of Gotham—

A agree on most matters

B are excited to see the king

C have a plan to deal with the king

D have trouble following directions

7 How would the play be different if the king told the story?

A The reader would understand why the king is upset.

B The reader would know why the men dislike the king.

C The reader would know why the king wants to go to the town.

D The reader would understand what the men plan to do to the king.

8 Why do you feel the author used the names Hodge, Podge, Nodge, and Scrodge? What do these names suggest about the characters? Use details from the play to support your answer.

9 At the opening of the play, the characters are cutting trees down. How does the author use dialogue to explain why the characters are doing this? Use details from the play to support your answer.

10 The play includes details that describe actions for characters to carry out. Give **two** examples of actions the king carries out in Scene I. Explain what each action shows about the king.

11 How did cutting down the trees in Scene I affect the king? Explain how the setting and the dialogue at the beginning of Scene II show the effect on the king. Use details from the play to support your answer.

12 At the end of Scene I, the king tells his soldier to give a message to the people of Gotham. Do the people of Gotham receive this message? Use details from the play to explain how you can tell.

13 Complete the chart below to summarize the **four** foolish things that the king observes in Scene II.

What the King Observes	Why It Is Foolish

14 Are the main characters really foolish or were they doing foolish things on purpose? Use at least **two** specific details from the play to support your conclusion.

Planning Space

You can write notes, make a list, or draw a chart to help plan your answer.

_____

_____

_____

_____

_____

_____

_____

_____

_____

_____

_____

_____

15 Explain why the king decided to let the people keep their noses. How did the actions of Hodge, Podge, Nodge, and Scrodge lead to this decision? Use details from the play to support your answer.

Planning Space

You can write notes, make a list, or draw a chart to help plan your answer.

_____

_____

_____

_____

_____

_____

_____

_____

_____

_____

_____

_____

Directions: Read the passage. Then answer the questions that follow it.

Living in a Wildlife Camp

By Claire J. Griffin

1 Meet 12-year-old Madison McNutt and 8-year-old Wilder McNutt. These two boys' parents are researchers who study wild dogs in Botswana. A typical day begins with the boys waking up and dressing in their tree house.

6:30 A.M. Eat Breakfast by the Fire

2 Madison and Wilder gather around the campfire with their parents, their teacher, and the other researchers, about 10 people in all. In summer, the weather is hot, but winter mornings can be cold. Peggy, the cook, can make anything over the open fire, even pancakes.

7:30 A.M. Look for Animal Tracks

3 The boys help look for animals near camp. They have two ways of doing this.

4 The first way is to look for tracks in the sand. Honey badgers, hyenas, or leopards might have visited camp in the night.

5 The second way of finding an animal is by radio. The researchers have fitted some wild animals with collars that give off radio signals. A tower near camp picks up the signals. Most of the animals (lions, wild dogs, and others) live in groups. If the researchers find one animal, they usually have found the whole group.

8:00 A.M. Read, Write, Dissect a Leopard

6   On weekday mornings, Madison and Wilder have classes. Usually, the boys do typical schoolwork. But sometimes they may take on something special, such as helping to dissect a leopard that died near camp.

7   Wilder says, "I liked the paws best. The pads were soft, but the claws were sharp. The paws were flexible, and if you squeezed them, you could make the toes move. It was kind of gross but also very cool."

8   Saturday or Sunday morning can mean a game drive, which is a trip in the open-topped Land Rover to observe wildlife. As long as the McNutts stay in the vehicle, they are safe, even from lions and leopards. No one knows why the animals don't attack. Maybe predators think humans are part of the Land Rover.

Hyenas

9   The boys and their parents often spot lions, leopards, cheetahs, hyenas, and wild dogs. They also see the animals that these predators eat—zebras, impalas, kudus, and warthogs.

10   Madison describes seeing a cheetah feeding with her two cubs. "We'd never seen cheetahs on a kill so close to the road and so easy to watch," he says. "The mother had killed a young impala. They were totally calm and didn't mind us watching."

12:45 P.M. Stop for Lunch

11   Peggy has made lasagna and fresh-baked bread. Delicious!

1:30 P.M. Have Fun, Play Games

12   In the afternoon, the boys enjoy some free time. They read, play Ping-Pong, or hang out with one of the camp visitors, such as a dwarf mongoose. They also make things. Madison recently surprised Peggy with a new dinner bell. Wilder likes to work on cars. Last year they helped build their tree house.

4:30 P.M. Search for More Wildlife

13   The boys like the Gomoti River at sunset, when the animals come to drink. As the sky turns rosy, elephants stand at the water's edge and snake their trunks into the water. One of them might raise its trunk and shower water over its giant head. The giraffes amble up and spread their stiff legs out to the sides so they can lower their heads and drink. Hundreds of water birds circle overhead. They call loudly and land on the water in a rush of beating wings.

6:30 P.M. Drive Home

14   Night has fallen by the time the family returns to camp. Sometimes their dad lets Madison drive the Land Rover.

7:00 P.M. Eat by the Fire

15   The evening meal might be spaghetti, pizza, chicken, or traditional Botswana food such as *seswaa* (beef stew) and *pap* (cornmeal mush, which they eat with their hands). Afterward, everyone sits around the fire and talks about the day.

8:30 P.M. Hit the Shower

16   The shower is outside, under a tree, behind reed walls. The water comes from a metal tank with a wood fire underneath. The water takes hours to get hot, but showering feels good after a long, dusty day.

9:00 P.M. Listen to Night Sounds

17   Wilder and Madison lie in their beds in the tree house, listening to the African night. They may hear the deep cough of a lion or the whoop of a hyena or the worried call of a wild dog that's separated from its pack. The brothers fall asleep under the star-filled African sky and dream of tomorrow's adventures.

Directions: Answer the following questions. If you need more space to write an answer, write your answer on your own paper.

1 Which meaning of the word *game* is used in paragraph 8?

   A willing and ready

   B brave and determined

   C a type of pastime

   D wild animals

2 The details in the last paragraph are used to suggest that the boys find living in the wildlife camp—

   A frightening.

   B boring.

   C challenging.

   D interesting.

3 The author organizes this article by—

   A explaining the effects of one event.

   B putting events in chronological order.

   C comparing one idea to several other ideas.

   D presenting a problem and offering a solution.

4 The author most likely uses headings to—

   A explain where events take place.

   B show readers what each section is about.

   C explain what is happening in the pictures.

   D show readers the meaning of unknown words.

5 How would the article be different if it were a first-hand account by Wilder?

A It would show how Wilder feels about his experiences.

B It would describe the things that Wilder learns.

C It would tell how Wilder helps his parents.

D It would explain where Wilder lives.

6 Read this dictionary entry.

> **track** \'trak\ *noun*
> 1. a footprint left on the ground 2. a path or trail along which something moves 3. a train of ideas 4. a sport performed on a running track

Which definition of *track* is used in paragraph 4?

A Definition 1

B Definition 2

C Definition 3

D Definition 4

7 Which word from paragraph 6 helps the reader understand the meaning of the word *typical*?

A weekday

B classes

C special

D camp

8 Describe the structure of the section titled "Look for Animal Tracks." How do the three paragraphs fit together? Use details from the article to support your answer.

9 One of the sections is titled "Read, Write, Dissect a Leopard." How does this title surprise the reader? What does the title suggest about how the boys' school day compares with typical school days? Use details from the article to support your answer.

10 What new information does Wilder's firsthand account in paragraph 7 give? What does his account suggest about how Wilder feels about his life? Use details from the article to support your answer.

11 Closely reread paragraph 13. The author chooses words to create a clear image of how each animal moves. Complete the chart by identifying the phrase that best shows how each animal moves. Describe what each phrase tells you about how the animal moves.

Animal	Language Used to Describe the Animal's Movement	What the Language Tells About How the Animal Moves
elephants		
giraffes		
water birds		

12 Why is fire important in the wildlife camp? Use at least **two** specific examples of how fire is used to support your answer.

13 Describe the structure of the whole article. How does the structure support the article's main purpose? Use details from the article to support your answer.

14 The section "Read, Write, Dissect a Leopard" includes quotes from both Wilder and Madison. In what main way does Madison sound different from Wilder? How do these quotes help show their different ages? Use details from the article to support your answer.

Planning Space

You can write notes, make a list, or draw a chart to help plan your answer.

_____

_____

_____

_____

_____

_____

_____

_____

_____

_____

_____

_____

_____

_____

15 The article is based around a day in the life of Madison and Wilder. How can you tell that the article does not describe one specific day? Explain why the author did not describe just one specific day. Use details from the article to support your answer.

Planning Space

You can write notes, make a list, or draw a chart to help plan your answer.

_____

_____

_____

_____

_____

_____

_____

_____

_____

_____

_____

_____

Directions: Read the following two poems. Then answer the questions that follow.

I Love the World

By Eileen Spinelli

1 I love the world when it is white,
when snowflakes fall in winter light
to cover everything in sight.

2 I love the world when it is blue—
a sweeping, rented beach-house view:
blue sea, blue sky, blue dolphins, too.

3 I love the world when it is green,
with fields of corn and climbing bean
and rows of peppers in between.

4 I love the world when it is red,
when scarlet leaves make mice a bed
and sunset crimsons overhead.

5 Each season's grace and gifts are mine—
the purple hills, the silver vine. . . .
And so, dear world,
this valentine.

I Like It When It's Mizzly

By Aileen Fisher

1   I like it when it's mizzly
and just a little drizzly
so everything looks far away
and make-believe and frizzly.

2   I like it when it's foggy
and sounding very froggy.
I even like it when it rains
on streets and weepy windowpanes
and catkins in the poplar tree
and *me*.

Directions: Use "I Love the World" to answer the following questions. If you need more space to write an answer, write your answer on your own paper.

1 How does the first-person point of view most affect the poem?

   A It allows the reader to form his or her own opinion.

   B It allows the reader to imagine the scenes described.

   C It allows the speaker to describe her feelings.

   D It allows the speaker to compare the seasons.

2 In the second stanza, the word *sweeping* is used to show that the view is—

   A beautiful.

   B wide.

   C bright.

   D clean.

3 Which line from the poem creates the clearest image of the color of something?

   A "when snowflakes fall in winter light"

   B "and rows of peppers in between."

   C "and sunset crimsons overhead."

   D "Each season's grace and gifts are mine—"

4 Which words rhyme in each stanza of "I Love the World"?

   A The last words in the first and third lines only

   B The last words in the first and second lines only

   C The last words in the second and third lines only

   D The last words in the first, second, and third lines

5 In which line from "I Love the World" does the speaker give human traits to something that is not human?

   A "when snowflakes fall in winter light"

   B "blue sea, blue sky, blue dolphins, too"

   C "and rows of peppers in between"

   D "when scarlet leaves make mice a bed"

6 Explain what the speaker means by "this valentine" in the last stanza of "I Love the World." How is the poem like a valentine? Use details from the poem to support your answer.

7 The ideas in the poem "I Love the World" are divided by topic. Explain how the rhyme pattern and the stanzas work together to achieve this.

8 The first four stanzas of "I Love the World" all begin by describing a color. Complete the chart below by listing the color and the season it represents. Then list **one** image described that represents the season.

Color	Season	Image

Directions: Use "I Like It When It's Mizzly" to answer the following questions. If you need more space to write an answer, write your answer on your own paper.

9 Read these lines from "I Like It When It's Mizzly."

> *I even like it when it rains*
> *on streets and weepy windowpanes*

The author most likely describes the windowpanes as "weepy" to suggest that the rain is—

A starting to come through the glass

B spotting the glass with drops of water

C running down the glass in little streams

D making a ticking sound against the glass

10 The poem includes some made-up words. What does the use of these words suggest about the age of the speaker? Use **two** specific examples of made-up words to support your answer.

11 The poem describes "weepy windowpanes." How does the word *weepy* help the reader imagine the raindrops? Use details from the poem to support your answer.

12 Does the rhythm of the poem suggest a calm or an excited feeling? Use details from the poem to support your conclusion.

Directions: Use both "I Love the World" and "I Like It When It's Mizzly" to answer the following questions.

13 Which of these best describes the point of view of the speakers in both "I Love the World" and "I Like It When It's Mizzly"?

 A Both speakers express fondness for nature.

 B Both speakers think all seasons are beautiful.

 C Both speakers wish for their favorite weather.

 D Both speakers remember playing outside as children.

14 What color would the speaker in "I Love the World" most likely use to describe the weather in "I Like It When It's Mizzly"?

 A Brown

 B Gray

 C Pink

 D Yellow

15 In both poems, the speaker describes how she feels about nature. Think about the ideas in each poem, the details included, and the techniques used. Write an essay comparing how each speaker presents her view. Include at least **two** similarities and **two** differences in your essay. Use information from both poems to support your answer.

Planning Space

You can complete the chart below to help plan your answer.

	I Love the World	I Like It When It's Mizzly
Ideas		
Details		
Techniques		

Directions: Read the following two passages. Then answer the questions that follow.

The Dolphin Who Loved Games

By Lyle Berg

1   Years ago, I studied biology—the science of living things. I was fascinated by dolphins. When I had the chance to work with scientists who studied how dolphins lived, swam, and talked to one another, I took it.

2   One day, a dolphin named Peg was brought to our facility and placed in what we called the Big Tank. It was a round pool of filtered salt water, about 60 feet across and 5 feet deep. Six other friendly dolphins lived in the Big Tank, but Peg seemed especially friendly. Whenever I was working around the tank, she would swim along the side, staying as close to me as she could.

Peg's Toy Ball

3   I wondered if she would like something to play with, so I went to a store and bought a yellow ball about the size of a soccer ball. The next morning, I tossed the ball into her pool. As soon as she saw it, she shot through the water and tucked the ball under her left pectoral fin—one of the two fins that dolphins have in front.

4   From that day on, she always had that yellow ball with her, and she always tucked it under the same fin. When I walked up to the tank, she would swim over, let the ball go, and use her long snout to flip it up for me to catch.

Race to the Ball

5   Peg loved that game, but there was another one she liked even better. My dog liked to play a game in which I would throw a ball and we would race each other to get it. The dog was much

faster and always got there first. I wanted to try this game with Peg, too.

6 The next time she tossed me the ball, I threw it to the far edge of her pool. Then I started to run around the edge of the pool as fast as I could.

7 She liked the game, but she played it differently than my dog did. Instead of going fast, she swam slowly across the pool, getting to the ball just before I did. Peg should have been able to get to her ball way ahead of me. She only had to swim across her tank and could hit speeds of up to 20 miles per hour. But I had to run all the way around the edge in my clumsy rubber boots. I wasn't nearly as fast.

8 I wondered, "Why didn't she swim faster? Was it more fun getting to the ball at the last second and swooshing it away just before I picked it up?"

9 But that wasn't all that was different. Peg didn't always get to the ball first. Once in a while, she let me get to the ball first. I

wondered why. The only thing I could think of was that she didn't want me to get discouraged and stop playing with her.

Playing with Gulls

10   Peg made up another game all by herself.

11   At feeding time, Peg would often save bits of fish and use them to play with the gulls hanging around the pool.

12   A few gulls always sat on the edge, hoping to pick up scraps of fish. The gulls stayed on the edge because if they landed in the water, the dolphins swam under them and tossed them into the air. (Today, gulls are kept away from dolphins in marine mammal facilities to protect the dolphins from a sick gull that might make them sick.)

13   To play her "Gull Game," Peg took a piece of fish in her teeth and, with a flick of her head, tossed it into the water, near one of the gulls. The gull would quickly lean out over the edge and reach down to get the food.

14   If the food landed too close to the gull, Peg shot over and grabbed the fish in her teeth before the gull could grab it. Then Peg backed up and tried again. If she got the distance just right, the gull would reach too far, lose its balance, and fall into the water with a *plop*. Peg always let the gull keep the fish and didn't toss the bird up in the air, but she did *chitter-chatter*. I supposed she was laughing. I know I was.

15   During my work at the facility, I never learned to speak "dolphin." But Peg and I had a lot of fun playing together, and the two of us seemed to communicate just fine.

Animals and Their Trainers: A Good Team

By Sara F. Shacter

1   Ever wish you could speak to a sparrow, chat with a cheetah, or babble to a baboon? Then think about becoming an animal trainer. Brett Smith is a trainer at Chicago's Lincoln Park Zoo. He says training animals is almost like talking to them.

2   In a zoo or aquarium, an animal and its trainer are a team. Trainers learn to read their animals' behavior to figure out what each animal wants and needs. Animals learn to cooperate with their teachers. This teamwork makes it possible for each animal to live comfortably and get the best care.

3   For everyone's safety, trainers need to teach animals how to behave during a checkup. Do visits to the doctor's office make you squirm? Imagine trying to examine a squirming, trumpeting elephant! Elephants learn how to place their feet so veterinarians can check them. Dolphins learn how to place their tails so veterinarians can take blood samples.

4   At some aquariums, dolphins are taught how to protect themselves from humans' mistakes. Sometimes people drop things into the dolphins' tank. In the water, a plastic bag looks a lot like a squid. But a dolphin could die if it eats the bag. So these dolphins are trained to bring stray objects to the trainers.

5 Because trainers and their animals spend so much time together, their bond of trust is strong. This bond helps trainers do important research. For example, a trainer might be able to get up close when a mother is feeding her new baby. That's something most wild animals wouldn't allow.

Fun and Rewards

6 How do trainers teach animals? Ken Ramirez is the head trainer at Chicago's John G. Shedd Aquarium. He says that animals and people learn best the same way: through fun and rewards.

7 Mr. Ramirez doesn't punish. He wants the animals to have a good time. When the animal does what it's supposed to do, it gets a reward. Often the reward is food, but it can be something else. Belugas (white whales), for example, love having their tongues tickled.

8   Trainers believe that it's also important to give animals the chance to play. New sights, sounds, and experiences keep animals' minds and bodies healthy. At the Shedd aquarium, dolphins enjoy watching their reflections in mirrors. One dolphin looks at herself for hours. At the Lincoln Park Zoo, lions play with piñatas. The lions rush up, smack their prey, and jump away. Once they're sure the piñatas won't fight back, the lions rip them open. They find the food or bone inside and make shredded paper their new toy.

9   Training animals takes time and patience, but the rewards are huge. Ken Ramirez says a trainer is an animal's "parent, doctor, playmate, and best friend." Animals may not speak our language, but they have much to tell us.

Who's Training Whom?

10   Ken Ramirez once worked with a dolphin that could always find a piece of trash in his tank, even when the pool looked clean. The dolphin earned a fish reward for each piece of trash he turned in.

11   Soon the trainers became suspicious. They began saving everything the dolphin found, from bags to newspaper scraps. When they noticed that the newspaper scraps fit together, they realized what was going on.

12   The dolphin had found a little nook in the tank, perfect for storing trash. When he wanted a snack, he'd grab some garbage and turn it in for a treat.

Directions: Use "The Dolphin Who Loved Games" to answer the following questions. If you need more space to write an answer, write your answer on your own paper.

1 Which phrase from the article uses language to show fast movement?

   A "swim along the side"

   B "tossed the ball"

   C "shot through the water"

   D "tucked the ball under"

2 Which sentence from "Race to the Ball" is a comparison?

   A "My dog liked to play a game in which I would throw a ball and we would race each other to get it."

   B "The next time she tossed me the ball, I threw it to the far edge of her pool."

   C "She liked the game, but she played it differently than my dog did."

   D "She only had to swim across her tank and could hit speeds of up to 20 miles per hour."

3 Based on the information in "Peg's Toy Ball," what part of a dolphin is a *snout*?

   A fin

   B flipper

   C tail

   D nose

4 In "The Dolphin Who Loved Games," how does the author organize the section "Race to the Ball"?

   A By comparing how a dolphin and a dog play the same game

   B By putting the events of the game in chronological order

   C By describing the effect the game has on the dolphin

   D By offering solutions to a problem with the game

5 In paragraph 15 of "The Dolphin Who Loved Games," which word helps the reader understand the meaning of the word *communicate*?

   A work

   B speak

   C fun

   D playing

6 How does the author's description of the "Gull Game" make it seem amusing? Describe at least **two** ways the author emphasizes the humor of the game. Use details from the passage in your response.

7 In the section "Race to the Ball," the author makes assumptions about why Peg does things. Describe **two** assumptions the author makes. Explain how you know that they are assumptions. Use details from the passage in your response.

Directions: Use "Animals and Their Trainers: A Good Team" to answer the following questions. If you need more space to write an answer, write your answer on your own paper.

8 In paragraph 11 of "Animals and Their Trainers: A Good Team," the word suspicious most closely means—

A   angry.

B   entertained.

C   proud.

D   questionable.

9 Read paragraph 2 of the article. Explain what the word *cooperate* means. Describe **two** details in the paragraph that help show the meaning of the word.

10 The article describes the purpose of training dolphins. Complete the graphic organizer below by listing **two** examples of problems and explaining how training the dolphin solves the problem.

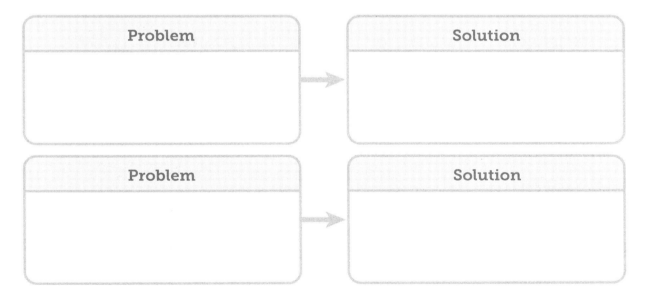

Problem	Solution

Problem	Solution

11 "Who's Training Whom?" is the title of the last section of the article. What does this title imply? Explain how it relates to the events described in the section. Use details from the section to support your answer.

12 Ken Ramirez states that animals are best trained using both fun and rewards. How is the training of the lions at Lincoln Park Zoo an example of using fun and rewards? Use details from the article to support your answer.

Directions: Use "The Dolphin Who Loved Games" and "Animals and Their Trainers: A Good Team" to answer the following question.

13 "The Dolphin Who Loved Games" and "Animals and Their Trainers: A Good Team" are different because—

A "Animals and Their Trainers: A Good Team " shows that animal trainers play with animals.

B "The Dolphin Who Loved Games" offers a first-hand account of working with animals.

C "Animals and Their Trainers: A Good Team " explains what animal trainers do.

D "The Dolphin Who Loved Games" describes where certain animals live.

14 Both "The Dolphin Who Loved Games" and "Animals and Their Trainers: A Good Team " use headings to—

A tells readers what information is in each section.

B offer readers extra information about a topic.

C describe the meaning of difficult words.

D call attention to important words.

15 Both articles describe how people work with and train dolphins. Compare the point of view of the two articles. Which point of view best shows the relationship that forms between dolphins and the people they work with? Which point of view best shows the purpose of forming these relationships? Use information from both articles to support your answer.

Planning Space

You can complete the chart below to help plan your answer.

	"The Dolphin Who Loved Games"	"Animals and Their Trainers: A Good Team"
What is the point of view?		
Does the point of view show the relationship between dolphins and people?		
Does the point of view show the purpose of forming the relationship?		

_____

_____

_____

_____

_____

_____

_____

_____

_____

_____

_____

_____

_____

_____

_____

_____

_____

_____

_____

_____

_____

_____

_____

Part C:

Integration of Knowledge and Ideas

Literary, Informational, and Paired Passages with Multiple Choice, Short Response, Extended Response, and Essay Questions

Reading Standards

R.4.7   Interpret information presented visually, orally, or quantitatively (e.g., in charts, graphs, diagrams, time lines, animations, or interactive elements on Web pages) and explain how the information contributes to an understanding of the text in which it appears. Make connections between the text of a story or drama and a visual or oral presentation of the text, identifying where each version reflects specific descriptions and directions in the text.

✓ **Informational**   ✓ **Literary**

R.4.8   Explain how an author uses reasons and evidence to support particular points in a text.

✓ **Informational**

R.4.9   Integrate information from two texts on the same topic in order to write or speak about the subject knowledgeably. Compare and contrast the treatment of similar themes and topics (e.g., opposition of good and evil) and patterns of events (e.g., the quest) in stories, myths, and traditional literature from different cultures.

✓ **Informational**   ✓ **Literary**

Instruction

Directions: Read the passage. The guides in the blue bar will help you focus on some of the important details. Then answer the questions that follow. These questions will also have guides to help you find the correct answers.

La Muerta: Godmother Death

A Play based on a Mexican Tale

Retold by Pat Betteley
Illustrated by Andouillette

Look at the title. Look at the illustrations. What do you think this play will be about?

CHARACTERS:

Narrator 1	Señora
Narrator 2	Holy Woman
Narrator 3	La Muerta
Antonio	Julio

1 Narrator 1: One day, a new son was born to Antonio, a poor Mexican peasant.

2 Antonio: Born on the Day of the Dead—that is a good sign. I have a feeling that this child will change everything for our family. I must find a madrina (godmother) who can offer him justice, mercy, and especially, power.

3 Narrator 1: So Antonio set off. Soon he came upon the señora who owned the hacienda (house) down the road, riding in a splendid carriage.

4 Señora: Antonio, why are you walking without your family today?

5   Antonio: A new child has been born to us this
very day.

6   Señora: Born on the Day of the Dead? It will surely
be a special child. My family is old and rich, and I
could give your child riches and power. I would
make a fine madrina.

Why is Antonio's child so unique?

7   Antonio: I am honored. You are indeed powerful, but
not just or merciful. While your children play with
golden toys, my children, so nearby, starve. My child
deserves more than you can offer.

8   Narrator 2: Antonio kept walking. Next he saw a holy
woman dressed in rags.

9   Holy Woman: Why do you walk alone, Antonio?

10   Antonio: A new child was born to me.

11   Holy Woman: I would make a fine madrina. I could
give your child justice and mercy.

12   Antonio: I am honored. But you are poor, and there
is no power in poverty. This child must have more
than you can provide.

13   Narrator 2: So Antonio continued on his way until
he saw a tall, thin woman wrapped in cloth that hid
even her mouth.

14   La Muerta: I know you have a new baby. I would
make a fine madrina. I could provide him with
justice, mercy, and power.

15   Antonio: And you are…?

16   La Muerta: La Muerta — Death.

17 Antonio: Then I know you are merciful because you end suffering. And you are just, taking life from the rich and the poor alike. And no power on earth can match yours. Yes, you will be a fine godmother to my child.

18 Narrator 3: Antonio's child Julio grew well and quickly. His madrina showed him the use of every healing herb in the woods. Soon Julio knew more about the healing powers of herbs than any doctor in the land.

19 La Muerta: Julio, I have a final gift for you. This pale yellow flower is called La Yerba de la Vida. You can use it to make a medicine that will bring the dying back to life. There is one condition, though. You may only give the medicine if I am at the foot of the bed of the dying one. If you see me at the head of the bed, do not give it, for I have come to claim my own.

20 Narrator 3: Julio went out into the world and healed the rich and poor alike. He became known as Julio de los Remedios.

21 Narrator 1: One day, the dying king offered half his kingdom to the person who could cure him. Ready to put an end to his family's poverty, Julio brought La Yerba de la Vida to the king's bedside. But La Muerta was standing sternly at the head of the bed.

22 Julio: (thinking quickly) The king needs air. Turn his bed so that his head is near the window. (to himself) And so Death is at the foot of his bed!

23 La Muerta: If you ever cheat me again, I will come for you.

Why does Antonio turn away other madrinas before accepting La Muerta?

What is the special power behind La Yerba de la Vida?

WORD HELP:

Julio de los Remedios means "Julius of the Remedies" in Spanish.

La Yerba de la Vida means "the herb of life" in Spanish.

24   Narrator 1: Now Julio moved into the court and fell in love with the king's daughter. One week before their wedding, the princess fell ill. Julio ran to her room with the medicine, but was horrified to see La Muerta at the head of her bed.

25   Julio: (thinking to himself) Surely my godmother will not carry out her threat when the dying one is my future wife.

26   Narrator 2: Julio turned the bed around so La Muerta was at the foot, and gave the medicine to the princess. When he looked up, his madrina was gone.

27   Narrator 2: A week later, Julio drifted off to sleep on his wedding night. La Muerta knocked at the door and led him to a huge underground cavern with thousands of lit candles. Some were flickering out, while others were bursting into flame.

28   La Muerta: These are the lights of people's lives. The candle over there with the sputtering flame is yours, Julio.

29   Julio: No, madrina. Show me mercy!

30   La Muerta: I have shown you mercy. This candle that is just flickering to life is the candle of your own child.

31   Julio: I am to be a father? Please, madrina, spare my life so I can raise my child!

32 La Muerta: I have shown you mercy and given you power. Now it is time to show you justice.

33 Narrator 1: La Muerta bent over and blew out the candle of Julio de los Remedios.

Why does La Muerta get so angry at Julio?

1 Read the following lines from the play.

> *Narrator 1: One day, a new son was born to Antonio, a poor Mexican peasant.*
>
> *Antonio: Born on the Day of the Dead – that is a good sign. I have a feeling that this child will change everything for our family.*

What is the purpose of these lines?

A to introduce the setting

B to introduce the importance of a particular character

C to introduce the solution to the problem

D to introduce the main characters

This is a **Making Text/Visual/Oral Connections** question. Look at where this information is presented in the play. What are these lines introducing?

2 Read the following lines from the play.

> *La Muerta: I have shown you mercy and given you power. Now it is time to show you justice.*

From these lines, what may happen next?

A La Muerta is going to kill Julio's child.

B La Muerta is going to let Julio live forever.

C La Muerta is going to bring Julio's killer to justice.

D La Muerta is going to kill Julio.

This is a **Making Text/Visual/Oral Connections** question. Think about how La Muerta would deliver these lines. What would her voice sound like?

3 What does the illustration on page 165 represent about this play?

A Antonio's new baby

B the Day of the Dead

C la yerba de la vida

D the different godmothers

This is a **Making Text/Visual/Oral Connections** question. Look at the graphic. What does it show you in regards to the lines of this play?

4 Read the following lines from the play.

> *Antonio's child Julio grew well and quickly...Soon Julio knew more about the healing powers of herbs than any doctor in the land.*

How would Julio now appear in a visual version of this play?

A like an old, wise man

B like a baby

C like a clever adult

D like an animal

This is a **Making Text/Visual/Oral Connections** question. If you are watching a play presented onstage and time passes, how would the character's appearances change?

5 Read the following lines from the play.

> *Señora: Born on the Day of the Dead? It will surely be a special child. My family is old and rich, and I could give your child riches and power. I would make a fine madrina.*

> *Antonio: I am honored. You are indeed powerful, but not just or merciful. While your children play with golden toys, my children, so nearby, starve. My child deserves more than you can offer.*

What do the lines suggest will happen next?

A Señora will get revenge on Antonio.

B Antonio will stop looking for a suitable godmother for his child.

C Señora will become the godmother for Antonio's child.

D Antonio will keep searching for a suitable godmother for his child.

This is a **Making Text/Visual/Oral Connections** question. Look at where this information is presented in the play. What is the next logical step that will happen in the play?

6 What would La Muerta's voice sound like in an oral reading of this play when she says, "If you ever cheat me again, I will come for you?"

A happy and cheery

B angry and threatening

C tired

D soft and whispery

This is a **Making Text/Visual/Oral Connections** question. Think about how La Muerta probably feels when she delivers this line.

7 What does La Muerta offer to provide Antonio's new baby?

A money, protection, and a job

B mercy and peace

C power, justice, and mercy

D nothing

This is a **Making Text/Visual/Oral Connections** question. What does La Muerta have to offer?

8 How does La Muerta show mercy? Use details from the play to support your answer.

This is a **Making Text Connections** question. Based on your reading of the passage, you can tell how La Muerta shows mercy based on what kind of character she is.

9 In line 23, La Muerta tells Julio, "If you ever cheat me again, I will come for you." What has Julio done that causes La Muerta to say this?

This is a **Making Text Connections** question. Julio does something in prior parts of the text to make La Muerta feel the way she does.

10 Describe two ways you can tell that "La Muerta: Godmother Death" is a play. Use specific examples from the play in your answer.

This is a **Genre** question. What is special about the way this passage is written that may indicate it is a play?

11 How does the La Yerba de la Vida fit into the overall theme and plot of this play?

This is a **Making Text/Visual/Oral Connections** question. La Yerba de la Vida is a specific flower that is common in Mexico. How does the author use this cultural information to help the reader understand its theme?

12 What is the meaning of the candles in the underground cavern? Use details from the play to support your answer.

This is a **Making Text/Visual/Oral Connections** question. Look back in the passage to see why and how these candles are used. How does the author use this cultural information to help the reader understand its theme?

13 Why does Julio think La Muerta might spare his life? Use details from the play to support your answer.

This is a **Making Text Connections** question. Based on La Muerta's prior actions, how does Julio feel about La Muerta?

14 This play is from the Mexican culture. In Greek mythology, the gods use the cutting of a thread to symbolize the end of a person's life. How is this similar to what is used in the Mexican culture? Use details from the passage to support your answer.

Planning Space

You can write notes, make a list, or draw a chart to help plan your answer.

This is a **Making Text/Visual/Oral Connections** question. You are comparing and contrasting Mexican culture VS Greek culture. What do you know, based on the play?

_____

_____

_____

_____

_____

_____

_____

_____

_____

_____

_____

15 The play begins with the line "Narrator 1: One day, a new son was born to Antonio, a poor Mexican peasant." Fill out the flow chart to describe the pattern, in order, of events that lead to La Muerta's final action at the end.

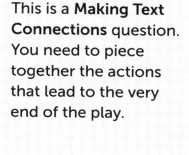

This is a **Making Text Connections** question. You need to piece together the actions that lead to the very end of the play.

Planning Space

Use the flow chart below to list the steps.

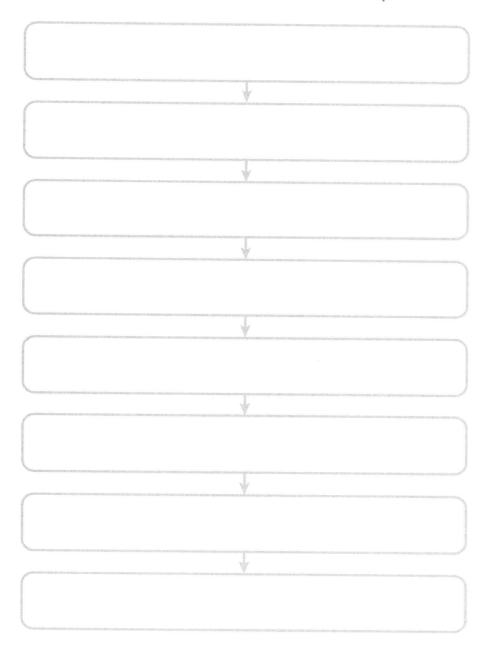

_____

_____

_____

_____

_____

_____

_____

_____

_____

_____

_____

_____

_____

Directions: Read the passage. The guides in the blue bar will help you focus on some of the important details. Then answer the questions that follow. These questions will also have guides to help you find the correct answers.

Fairy Tale Science

By Charlene Brusso, Art by Dave Clark

Could anyone really sleep for a hundred years? Dance in glass slippers? Get gold eggs from a goose? And could science ever make magic come true?

Look at the title. Look at the illustrations. What do you think this passage will be about?

1   Wouldn't it be nice if magic were real? Then again, a lot of things you do every day would seem quite magical to the people who made up Cinderella and Sinbad. Hundreds of years ago, the idea of seeing what was happening far away, talking to someone in another town, or traveling through the air was pure fantasy. Yet now people do those things all the time. Science has made these dreams real. So what else could science do?

Sleepy Beauty

2   Have you ever wished you could cast spells—just say something and have it come true? Maybe it's just as well you can't, or the next time you borrowed your sister's skates without asking, she might put you to sleep for 100 years, like Sleeping Beauty.

3   Could anyone really sleep for 100 years? Probably not. The daily cycle of sleep and waking is programmed into every cell in your body and is hard to disrupt. But some animals do take very long naps.

Bears, groundhogs, mice, and snakes can sleep for months at a time when they hibernate through the winter. A hibernating animal slows down its breathing and heart rate, lowers its body temperature, and doesn't eat or drink. Then when the weather warms, it wakes up. Seeds and some tiny insects can dry themselves out and remain dormant for many years at a time.

4   If scientists can figure out how animals hibernate, maybe one day people could hibernate too. This would be great for astronauts, who could sleep through long space voyages. Hibernation tricks might also help doctors slow disease.

5   But even hibernating animals still grow older—so if a future Sleeping Beauty ever did manage to hibernate for 100 years, she might wake up as Sleeping Grandma.

How do certain animals hibernate for long periods of time?

Glass Slipper

6   They might look sparkly, but would you really want shoes made of glass? It's hard, slippery, and likely to

shatter at the first foot-tap. But if a modern-day Cinderella has her heart set on a pair of glass slippers, science has been catching up.

7   Glassmakers have discovered ways to make glass extra tough by heating and quickly cooling it, or by tweaking the glass's chemical recipe. This toughened, or tempered, glass is strong and scratch-proof. It can even be made a bit bendy. And when it does break, it shatters into small chunks instead of knife-sharp shards.

8   You don't have to go to a ball to see this magical glass—it's all around you in car windows, refrigerator shelves, cell phones, and computers. And who knows? Maybe someday even shoes.

Jumping Gems

9   In the story "Toads and Diamonds," a fairy rewards a kind girl with a spell that makes gems fall from her mouth when she speaks (her mean sister gets toads). That's much less work than digging them out of the ground!

10   We're unlikely to ever be able to pull gems from thin air. But scientists can grow gems in a laboratory.

11   To grow gems, scientists melt the mineral ingredients of the gemstone in a hot furnace, or with lasers. Then they let them slowly cool to form crystals. Gems were first grown this way in the late 1800s. These gems are identical to natural gems—and alas, nearly as expensive.

12 Lab-grown sapphire is used in watches and computers, and to make spaceship windows. Sapphire is almost as hard as diamond—and much harder than glass.

What is different about gems grown in a lab than real life gems?

Spinning Gold

13 If you can make gems out of powdered rock, could you ever spin gold out of straw, like Rumpelstiltskin?

14 When chemists make sapphire in a lab, they have to start with the ingredients of sapphire (aluminum and oxygen) first. Then they fuse them into sapphire.

15 But unlike sapphire, gold isn't a combination of different minerals. It's an element. That means it contains only one kind of atom—gold atoms. And atoms can't be changed, except inside stars (or nuclear reactors). So it's not really possible to make gold. Instead, the trick is to find it.

16 Where do you start looking? Scientists have discovered gold hiding in some surprising places— like seawater. Chemists estimate there are about 8 million tons of gold dissolved in seawater around the

Why is it so hard to find pure gold on Earth?

world. Unfortunately, Earth's oceans are huge, so the gold is spread thin—only a speck in a ton of water. It costs more to get the gold out of the water than the gold is worth. So, for now, Rumpelstiltskin can keep his corner on the fairy tale gold market.

Talk to the Animals

17 Where would all those lost princesses be without their kind animal helpers? And how convenient that they all speak English.

18 In the real world, talking to animals isn't quite so easy—yet. But scientists are making a lot of progress. The first lesson is that animals don't talk like humans. They communicate with gestures and smells as well as sounds.

19 And scientists are beginning to crack the code. Soon you may be able to tell just what bird calls, deer tail wags, elephant rumbles, and dolphin whistles are really saying. The next step is learning to talk back.

What is different about the way a bird talks from the way a human talks?

20 Of course, even if we learn to talk to animals, that doesn't mean animals think like people. They have very different minds. They're more likely to be saying "This is my tree, back off!" than giving directions to the nearest castle.

Let Down Your Hair

21 Poor Rapunzel, imprisoned in a tower, must lower her long braid to let visitors in. But how likely is this? Could hair really hold up a prince?

22 Surprisingly, yes! And you don't even need any magic. Plain old hair is quite strong stuff. A

WRONG

single strand can hold 3 ounces (100 g), the weight of four mice. And an average head has about 120,000 hairs. All those hairs braided together could hold a couple of elephants. A prince? No problem.

23 However, Rapunzel would be wise to tie her braid to the bedpost or a sturdy hook before letting someone climb it, or she'd get a painful hair-pull and a very sore neck.

24 Unfortunately, in real life human hair only grows a few feet long, at most. The longest hair ever recorded was about 18 feet (6 meters). That's pretty long for hair—but pretty short for a tower.

Super Strength

25 Long before comic book superheroes, lucky younger sons in fairy tales had magic potions, flying capes, belts of strength, and boots of speed to give them super-powers. So just how super can you get?

26 Alas, there's no magic potion that can make you strong or fast. Muscles grow strong by being used, period. But the human body can get a boost from some modern machines.

27 Mechanical exoskeletons are a little like wearing a robot. Computer-controlled motors sense your movements and move the exoskeleton's arms and legs to match. But because the suit's arms and legs are metal and motor-powered, they can be much stronger than your own muscles. And they never get tired. Some exoskeletons are used in factories to carry heavy loads or get around quickly. Other models can help injured or disabled people walk with just small gestures. That's pretty super!

How is science trying to make people stronger and faster?

Up, Up, and Away

28 So how about wings, or a nice broomstick? Will people ever be able to fly?

29 Inventors have been tinkering with one-person flying machines for many, many years, though none are quite ready for everyday wear. The Martin Jetpack, made by a company in New Zealand, looks like a backpack with two big fans. It can fly 46 miles (74 km) per hour—though not quite as elegantly as a broomstick.

30 One curious engineer has even made a carpet fly—or at least, a placemat. His "carpet" is two small sheets of different kinds of plastic stuck together. Electricity from a small battery makes the sheets vibrate at different rates, giving them a ripply motion. That's enough to make the light mat "swim" through the air like a ray over the ocean floor. Alas, to carry you this flying sheet would have to be the size of a football field. But it might be useful for exploring Mars someday.

Invisibility Cloak

31   It's always handy, when sneaking into an ogre's castle, to have an invisibility cloak, helmet, or ring that lets you walk unseen.

32   And you'll be glad to know that scientists are hard at work on a real invisibility cloak. It uses tiny antennas to channel light around an object, like water flowing around a rock in a stream. So far, it's more like a box than a cloak, and they've only managed to hide very small objects. But someday, hide-and-seek may never be the same.

33   Another way to go invisible is to camouflage yourself so you look exactly like your background. Some animals are quite good at this. Though it doesn't exist yet, it's possible that someday futuristic fabric will be able to see what's behind you and change to match.

Why aren't the flying "carpet" and the invisibility cloak ready for every day human use yet?

1 Read this sentence from the passage.

> *"Hundreds of years ago, the idea of seeing what was happening far away, talking to someone in another town, or traveling through the air was pure fantasy."*

What is the main reason the author describes these ideas of the past as "pure fantasy"?

A   Those ideas were ones that could never happen, no matter what.

B   Those ideas were ones the author thought were bad ideas.

C   Those ideas weren't possible many years ago.

D   Those ideas were ones that the author came up with.

This is a **Reasons and Evidence** question. You are looking for particular reasons an author chooses to make a particular point.

2 Which sentence in the first section is most important to the main idea?

A   "So what else could science do?"

B   "Yet now people do those things all the time."

C   "Wouldn't it be nice if magic were real?"

D   "Then again, a lot of things you do every day would seem quite magical to the people who made up Cinderella and Sinbad."

This is a **Reasons and Evidence** question. First, identify the main point of this section. Then, look for ways the author supports this point.

3 Why does the author choose to include an illustration of a bear in the section "Sleepy Beauty?"

A   Bears hibernate similar to the way Sleeping Beauty does.

B   Bears often works as doctors to princesses.

C   Bears enjoy healing people.

D   Bears never sleep for long periods of time.

This is an **Interpret Visual Information** question. How does the author connect what is in the illustration to meaning in the text?

4 In the section "Jumping Gems", the author mentions an example of an outside tale called "Toads and Diamonds." Why does the author choose to include mention of this story?

   A to show how misbehaving children get punished

   B to describe how frogs and toads get taken by children

   C to warn readers that if you misbehave, you will pay the price

   D to contrast a fictional way of receiving gems with a real-life way

This is a **Compare and Contrast Texts** question. Why would the author choose to include outside information?

---

5 In the illustration on page 180 by the section "Spinning Gold," why do you think the girl in the picture looks unhappy?

   A Gold can be created because it is made of multiple elements.

   B Both sapphire and gold can be created because they are made of multiple elements.

   C Sapphire, which is made of one type of element, must be found.

   D It is actually impossible to spin gold; it must be found in nature.

This is an **Interpret Visual Information** question. How does the author connect what is in the illustration to meaning in the text?

6 Which sentence from the section "Let Down Your Hair" is best represented by the illustrations on page 181 and 182? (the picture of the prince pulling on Rapunzel's hair incorrectly and correctly)

    A "However, Rapunzel would be wise to tie her braid to the bedpost…or she'd get a very painful hair-pull and a very sore neck."

    B "The longest hair ever recorded was about 18 feet (6 meters)."

    C "A single strand can hold 3 ounces (100 g), the weight of four mice."

    D "All those hairs braided together could hold a couple of elephants."

> This is an **Interpret Visual Information** question. How does the author connect what is in the illustration to meaning in the text?

7 Read these sentences from the section "Invisibility Cloak."

> *"And you'll be glad to know that scientists are hard at work on a real invisibility cloak. It uses tiny antennas to channel light around an object, like water flowing around a rock in a stream."*

How does the author best support the idea that water flowing around a rock in a stream is similar to light being channeled around an object with small antennas?

    A In this case, light can go through an object and water can go through a rock.

    B Neither light or water, in this case, can go through the thing they are being routed around.

    C While water, in this case, can flow through a rock, light cannot go through the object.

    D Light can flow through a rock, in this case, and water can flow through an object.

> This is **a Reasons and Evidence** question. First, identify the main point the author is trying to make in these sentences. Then, look for ways the author supports this point.

8 Why is the article called "Fairy Tale Science"? And how does the title relate to the rest of the article? Use details from the passage in your response.

This is a **Making Text Connections** question. Does the author use fairy tales in this article? What do you learn?

9 Read this sentence from the passage.

"If scientists can figure out how animals hibernate, maybe one day people could hibernate too."

What reasons or evidence does the author use to provide support for or add to this point? Use details from the passage in your response.

This is a **Reasons and Evidence** question. How does the author elaborate on the point made in the sentence?

10 Read this sentence from the passage.

> *"Glassmakers have discovered ways to make glass extra tough by heating and quickly cooling it, or by tweaking the glass's chemical recipe."*

What reasons or evidence does the author use to provide support for or add to this point? Use details from the passage in your response.

This is a **Reasons and Evidence** question. How does the author elaborate on the point made in the sentence?

---

11 Read this sentence from the passage.

> *"But scientists can grow gems in a laboratory."*

What reasons or evidence does the author use to provide support for or add to this point? Use details from the passage in your response.

This is a **Reasons and Evidence** question. In this instance, the sentence is the main point. Using the surrounding details in the passage, it is your job to explain the evidence behind this point.

12 Read this sentence from the passage.

> *"Plain old hair is quite strong stuff."*

What reasons or evidence does the author use to provide support for or add to this point? Use details from the passage in your response.

This is a **Reasons and Evidence** question. How does the author elaborate on the point made in the sentence?

---

13 Read this sentence from the passage.

> *"One curious engineer has even made a carpet fly—or at least, a placemat."*

What reasons or evidence does the author use to provide support for or add to this point? Use details from the passage in your response.

This is a **Reasons and Evidence** question. First, identify the main point the author is trying to make in this sentence. Then, look for ways the author supports this point.

14 From the section called "Spinning Gold," explain how scientists might be able to get gold out of ocean water. Use details from the passage in your response.

This is a **Reasons and Evidence** question. Read the sub-section "Spinning Gold" to look for possible ways to obtain gold from the ocean. Is this an easy task?

Planning Space

You can write notes, make a list, or draw a chart to help plan your answer.

_____

_____

_____

_____

_____

_____

_____

_____

_____

_____

_____

_____

15 Choose 3 sections of this article to read in more depth. For each of the 3 sections, answer these questions: What is the main point? What reasons and evidence does the author use to support the main idea?

This is a **Reasons and Evidence** question. To answer this question, you need to gather three main points, and provide evidence to support each point.

Planning Space

You can complete the chart below to help plan your answer.

Section Title	Main Point	Reasons and Evidence
1)		
2)		
3)		

_____

_____

_____

_____

_____

_____

_____

_____

_____

_____

_____

_____

Independent Practice

Directions: Read the passage. Then answer the questions that follow it.

2,000-Year-Old Homework!

Unroll a wad of paper and discover the secrets of ancient Egypt.

By Joli Allen

1 Dr. Todd Hickey opens a rusted tin box filled to the brim with tattered pieces of 2,000-year-old paper from Egypt. Dr. Hickey, a papyrologist (pap-eh-ROL-ah-jist), is excited about this rare type of treasure. It isn't covered in gold, but it is indeed priceless. That's because those tattered pieces of paper are papyrus. Papyrus tells us much about the secrets of life in ancient Egypt.

2 The Egyptians made this paper from papyrus plants that grew near the Nile River. Before papyrus, Egyptians mostly used copper chisels to carve words called hieroglyphs into stone. Papyrus made writing easier.

Writing to Go

3 With papyrus, Egyptians could now write signs and symbols using brushes, reed pens, and ink made from soot scraped out of cooking vessels and oil lamps. And they could take their writing wherever they went.

4 Dr. Hickey has already studied hundreds of the papyri. Some contain spells that the Egyptians wrote down and carried with them. They believed spells gave them magical protection or

power. Other papyri give directions for making powerful medicine. Archaeologists even found 2,000-year-old homework. A schoolboy had copied his lesson over and over with a reed quill.

From Trash to Treasure

5   When papyri weren't needed anymore for writing, they were tossed in the trash. The Egyptians reused these unwanted papyri to make papier-mâché. They shaped masks for human mummies or used the papyri to wrap animal mummies.

6   "Think of it as the ancient Egyptians' form of recycling," says Dr. Hickey.

7   Dr. Hickey needs to uncover valuable writings in the waste paper. And that is no easy task. It can take days to unroll just one wad of paper. First it is dampened to help it soften and relax. Then the paper is unrolled a bit. Dirt and gunk are carefully scraped off. The papyrologists must be careful not to scrape away the ink or paint underneath the dirt. The paper is unrolled a bit more. When the papyrus is completely unrolled, papyrologists look for torn pieces that fit together.

8   After the pieces are joined, is the job finished? No. The secrets from the past are still hidden, because words are missing from the worn bits of papyrus. The handwriting is faded and in ancient languages.

It's All Greek to Me

9   When Dr. Hickey decodes papyri, he needs to know other languages besides Egyptian. Ancient Egypt was ruled by the Greeks and Romans at different times, so he has to read and think in Greek and Latin.

10   Once he figures out what a sentence means, he tries to guess what the missing words or letters are in the holes of the papyrus.

11   "It's a challenge, but it is not impossible for papyrologists," Dr. Hickey says. "H—e would lead me to think 'horse' in some contexts, 'house' in others."

12   History leaps to life from each repaired papyrus. Dr. Hickey and other papyrologists found a police report to a royal scribe about a missing person. It reads: "On the 5th of the present month when patrolling the fields near the village ... I learn from the villagers that Theodotos son of Dositheos, having set out in that direction, has not yet returned. I make this report." The reporter also says that he found clues, but not the missing person.

13   Another piece of papyrus gave the dinner menu for a town's sacred crocodiles. The crocodiles were to be served meat, wine, and honey.

14   Some papyri give archaeologists a good idea of what Egyptians read for fun. They enjoyed adventure stories, poetry, plays, and myths.

15   It will take years for Dr. Hickey to study all the papyri in the tin box. He picks up a completed papyrus covered in protective glass. The writing on the papyrus forms a triangle, and the words can be read in several directions. It says the Greek nonsense phrase for a magical spell— similar to *abracadabra*. Too bad it can't be used to make all the papyrus bits in the tin box fall together instantly. But we can look forward to learning more about Egyptian life as each piece is connected.

Directions: Answer the following questions. If you need more space to write an answer, write your answer on your own paper.

1 Read this sentence from paragraph 1.

"It isn't covered in gold, but it is indeed priceless."

What is the main reason the author describes the papyrus as "priceless"?

A It is a form of trash.

B It contains valuable information.

C It is difficult to find.

D It dates back thousands of years.

2 Which sentence in the first section is most important to the main idea of the article?

A "Papyrus tells us much about the secrets of life in ancient Egypt."

B "The Egyptians made this paper from papyrus plants that grew near the Nile River."

C "Before papyrus, Egyptians mostly used copper chisels to carve words called hieroglyphs into stone."

D "Papyrus made writing easier."

3 The author of the article claims that tattered pieces of papyrus are "priceless." Which sentence from the article best supports this claim?

A Some contain spells that the Egyptians wrote down and carried with them.

B The Egyptians reused these unwanted papyri to make papier-mâché.

C History leaps to life from each repaired papyrus.

D Another piece of papyrus gave the dinner menu for a town's sacred crocodiles.

4 The picture of the box of tattered papyrus on page 195 helps support which idea from the article?

   A Piecing papyrus together can take years.

   B Finding pieces of papyrus to study is rare.

   C Reading pieces of repaired papyrus is difficult.

   D Writing became easier with the invention of papyrus.

5 The cartoons included with the article are used to make the article more—

   A dangerous.

   B easy.

   C interesting.

   D fun.

6 The author most likely describes how papyrus is unrolled to support the point that—

   A ancient papyrus is delicate.

   B working with papyrus is difficult.

   C words on papyrus may be nonsense.

   D writings on papyrus are in many languages.

7 If Dr. Hickey wrote this article, what information could he give readers that a secondhand author could not?

   A How most pieces of papyrus are usually found

   B What people have learned by studying papyrus

   C How it feels when repairing papyrus is a success

   D What a person must do to begin studying papyrus

8 How did using papyrus instead of stone make writing easier for the Egyptians? Use **two** details from the article to support your answer.

9 The article explains that it can "take days to unroll just one wad of paper." Complete the chart below to show the steps taken to unroll a wad of paper.

> The paper is dampened a little.

↓

>

↓

>

↓

> The paper is unrolled completely.

↓

>

10 How does the photograph of the papyrus on page 195 help show the difficult work that Dr. Hickey does? Use details from the article to support your answer.

11 The author includes illustrations to represent things that were learned about how the Egyptians lived. Choose **three** illustrations from the article. Describe what the illustration shows and what finding about Egyptian life it represents.

Description of the Illustration	The Finding About Egyptian Life Represented

12 Do you feel that the illustrations in the article make the papyrus findings seem important or unimportant? Use information from the article to support your conclusion.

13 Explain why Dr. Hickey needs to know Egyptian, Greek, and Latin languages. Use at least **two** details from the article to support your answer.

14 The papyrus contains valuable information, but it is not easy to obtain the information. Describe at least **two** challenges that make analyzing the papyrus difficult. Explain how each challenge can be overcome. Use information from the article to support your answer.

Planning Space

You can complete the chart below to help plan your answer.

Challenges that Make Analyzing the Papyrus Difficult	How the Challenge Is Overcome

_____

_____

_____

_____

_____

_____

_____

_____

_____

_____

_____

_____

_____

15 Scientists like Dr. Todd Hickey study papyrus to learn about life in ancient Egypt. Explain why Dr. Hickey studies papyrus. Give **three** examples of things that Dr. Hickey has learned by studying papyrus. Use information from the article to support your answer.

Planning Space

You can write notes, make a list, or draw a chart to help plan your answer.

Independent Practice

Directions: Read the following two passages. Then answer the questions that follow.

Alexander's Astounding World Feat

By Bradford H. Robie

1   "This is amazing," Alexander told his sister, Amy. "The record for eating hard-boiled eggs is 34 eggs in 30 minutes." He was reading *The Astounding Book of World Feats* by Captain Neville Puffer.

2   "That's disgusting," Amy said.

3   "Someone else ate 51 hot dogs in 12 minutes," Alexander continued.

4   Amy shuddered. "Isn't there any *useful* information? Like the record for running a mile?"

5   Alexander flipped through the pages. "Horatio Hopper skipped rope for 34 hours, stopping only once for a milkshake."

6   Amy shook her head.

7   "I'm going to set a world record, too," Alexander announced.

8   Amy laughed. "Which one? Not making your bed for 30 days in a row?"

9   But Alexander was serious about getting into *The Astounding Book of World Feats*. It was just a matter of *how*.

10 "I know!" he said. "I bet I can seesaw longer than anyone."

11 He checked the book and groaned when he read that a girl from Spain had teeter-tottered for 72 hours. What else could he do?

12 Some business cards lay on the kitchen table. Dad had a business card, and so did Mom. Why not collect business cards and assemble the world's largest collection? "That's it!" he said.

13   Alexander wasted no time in getting cards from his parents, the man painting their house, the neighbors, and the woman who delivered the newspaper. By the end of the week, he had 17 business cards.

14   "Hardly a world record," said Amy.

15   As Alexander thumbed through the Sunday paper, an idea hit him. He called his uncle Dex, who was a newspaper reporter.

16   "I'll get a short item in the paper tomorrow," Uncle Dex promised. And he did.

BOY WANTS BUSINESS CARDS

17   If Alexander Wells has his way, he'll soon be listed in *The Astounding Book of World Feats* for amassing the world's largest collection of business cards. To help, send *your* card to Alexander at the following address ...

18   The next day, 5 business cards arrived in the mail. And the day after that, 10. Then 35.

19   "Nice," Alexander said as he shuffled the cards in his hands.

20   Other newspapers picked up the story. In a few weeks, sacks of business cards were coming in from all over the state, from all sorts of people: lawyers, plumbers, engineers, musicians, gardeners, accountants.

21   Alexander soon ran out of space in his bedroom to store the cards. Holding a box of them, he knocked on Amy's door. "Can I put some in here?"

22 "No way," Amy said.

23 So he accumulated them in the attic; he gathered them in the garage. In just three months, his collection grew to more than a million!

24 Uncle Dex wrote a follow-up story: "Boy Collects a Million-Plus Business Cards." It included a picture of Alexander surrounded by his collection. Alexander sent this story to *The Astounding Book of World Feats* along with an official entry form.

25 And finally, he received what he'd been hoping for:

> *Dear Alexander,*
>
> *It is my pleasure to notify you of your record for the world's largest collection of business cards. Your accomplishment will appear in the next edition of* The Astounding Book of World Feats. *Also, you will receive a free trip to our annual awards ceremony.*
>
> *Sincerely,*
>
> *Captain Neville Puffer*

26 "I made it!" Alexander shouted. "I'm in the book!"

27 Amy read the letter, shaking her head. Then she patted her brother's back. "Didn't I always say you could do it?"

28 "Alexander," said his dad, "what will you do with all of those cards?"

29 Alexander asked Uncle Dex to write a final story announcing the record and asking people to stop sending cards. But the cards kept coming! The awards ceremony was held in a fancy hotel. Among the people at Alexander's table were Stringbean Sally, the world's tallest woman, and Ear-to-Ear Lear, the man with the world's widest smile. Next to Alexander sat a girl named Emily, who'd built the tallest replica of the Eiffel Tower with Popsicle sticks.

30 "What are you planning to do next?" Alexander asked Emily.

31 "Have you heard of the Leaning Tower of Pisa?"

32 Alexander nodded. "It's in Italy."

33 "I'd like to build a huge one out of playing cards." Emily sighed. "But it will take forever to collect the cards."

But it will take forever to collect the cards.

34 Alexander grinned. "Have you considered using business cards?"

Don't Try This at Home!

35 In real life, *Guinness Book of World Records* eliminated its "collected cards" category after a similar quest led to a huge amount of unwanted mail.

Running Rabbit
A Kumeyaay Folktale

Retold by Jeannie Beck

1   There was once a rabbit who was known to be the fastest rabbit in the world. The elders often spoke of this rabbit whenever a young boy came of age and it was time to test his hunting skills.

2   One small boy, who had heard the tale of this rabbit many times, decided that he would be the one to finally bring him in. As the years passed and the boy came of age, still no one had managed to bag Running Rabbit.

3   The elders cheered the boy on as he carved his first bow and arrow. He was given three days to hunt the rabbit. It was known that this rabbit always stayed in a certain flat area that was at least a mile long. It was here that the boy waited until he saw Running Rabbit.

4   "I have waited for you for a long time, and now you are old and it is time for you to leave this world," the boy said to the rabbit as he drew back his arrow. But by the time the arrow had left the bow, the rabbit had disappeared.

5   "That rabbit doesn't seem to get older, he just gets faster," the boy said to himself.

6   As night fell, the boy returned to camp, hearing the elders cheering his arrival because they had thought for sure that he would be the one to bring in the tricky old rabbit.

7   The boy did not hunt the next day, but instead searched for the strongest, straightest greasewood plant. From this plant he formed the sleekest arrow. Then he found the healthiest, most powerful elderberry tree from which he carved his new bow.

8   The boy decorated his new tools with elegant feathers from the magical flicker bird. Finally he shaped the sharpest, longest arrowhead, creating the least amount of wind resistance. When all was prepared, he fell asleep satisfied.

9   The next morning the boy returned to the flat and waited with complete confidence for Running Rabbit. As he strained his eyes to see through the early morning mist, he spied a streak of dust cutting through the fog. There he was!

10 The boy drew back his bow, and as the arrow left, so did the rabbit, who was showing off his fast running. About a mile away, the boy could see a large dark cloud rising up from the meadow.

11 When he reached the end of the flat, the boy saw a strange thing. There was his arrow, with the flicker feathers flying in the breeze, pinning a rabbit's fur to the ground. But where was Running Rabbit? The boy searched the meadow for hours before finally returning to camp with just the rabbit's soft coat. The elders thought the boy had made rabbit stew before returning home, so no one ever asked.

12 But the truth was, instead of running away from the boy, the rabbit had been showing off, and when he jumped so high and fast he ran into the arrow's path and got skinned. Running Rabbit narrowly escaped with his life, but not before losing his beautiful coat.

13 The naked rabbit was so embarrassed that he had to hide until he grew a new coat, and from then on he was shy like all the other rabbits.

Directions: Use "Alexander's Astounding World Feat" to answer the following questions. If you need more space to write an answer, write your answer on your own paper.

1 What does paragraph 17 of the story represent?

A a flyer Alexander put up

B an advertisement in a newspaper

C a business card Alexander received

D an article from the record book

2 Why does the author include the last paragraph?

A to summarize the information in the story

B to give a warning related to the topic of the story

C to explain that the events described did not really happen

D to encourage readers to choose a different record to break

3 Which part of "Alexander's Astounding World Feat" is shown in the illustration on page 209?

A Alexander feeling crowded by all the business cards.

B Alexander figuring out what world record he will set.

C Alexander talking about world records with his sister.

D Alexander finding a new use for all the business cards.

4 What does the section "Don't Try This at Home!" in "Alexander's Astounding World Feat" tell the reader?

A That Alexander's task was not easy

B How the story should have ended

C The correct way to start their own collection

D That the story is fiction

5 Look closely at the illustration on page 208. Complete the chart below by listing **two** more details in the illustration and explaining what each detail shows.

Detail	What the Detail Shows
The sister has her mouth covered.	She does not take her brother's goal seriously.

6 In paragraph 25, the author includes the letter Alexander received to show he had broken the record. Why do you think the author included the letter instead of just stating that Alexander received it? Use details from the story to support your answer.

7 Explain the meaning of paragraphs 33 and 34. What do they suggest will happen next? Use details from the story to support your answer.

Directions: Use "Running Rabbit" to answer the following questions. If you need more space to write an answer, write your answer on your own paper.

8 How does the illustration on page 211 help the reader's understanding?

    A It explains what happens to the rabbit in the end.

    B It makes the boy seem like a skilled rabbit hunter.

    C It explains why the boy wants to catch the rabbit.

    D It makes catching the rabbit seem like a huge task.

9 Describe **two** ways you can tell that "Running Rabbit" is a folktale. Use specific examples in your answer.

10 One of the themes of the story is about the dangers of showing off. Explain how the folktale communicates this message. Use details from the story to support your answer.

11 The illustration shows the rabbit as very large compared to the boy. Why do you think the rabbit was shown as large? Use details from the story to support your conclusion.

Directions: Use both "Alexander's Astounding World Feat" and "Running Rabbit" to answer the following questions.

12 What message do "Alexander's Astounding World Feat" and "Running Rabbit" share?

A Be kind to others.

B Look on the bright side.

C Always follow your dreams.

D Spend time with your family.

13 How are the quests in both stories alike?

A Both boys build tools to help them.

B Both boys get help from other people.

C Both boys receive an award at the end.

D Both boys make plans to reach their goals.

14 Both "Alexander's Astounding World Feat" and "Running Rabbit" are made-up stories. Explain which story you found the least realistic. Use examples from both stories to support your answer.

Planning Space

You can complete the chart below to help plan your answer.

Features of "Alexander's Astounding World Feat" that Are Not Realistic	Features of "Running Rabbit" that Are Not Realistic

_____

_____

_____

_____

_____

_____

_____

_____

_____

_____

_____

_____

15 Both stories describe a main character who has a goal. Compare the goals of the two characters and how they achieve their goals. Use details from both stories to support your answer.

Planning Space

You can complete the chart below to help plan your answer.

	Alexander	Boy from "Running Rabbit"
What is the goal?		
How hard is the goal to achieve?		
How does the character try to achieve the goal?		
Is the goal achieved?		

Directions: Read the passage. Then answer the questions that follow it.

Flying Circles Around Mercury

By Ken Croswell, Ph.D.

1   Giant craters, steep cliffs, ancient volcanoes, extreme heat and cold: welcome to mysterious Mercury.

2   Mercury is the closest planet to the Sun, and much of it is unexplored.

3   "Mercury is one of the big gaps in our knowledge of the solar system," says Robert Strom at the University of Arizona.

4   In 1974 and 1975, a spacecraft named *Mariner 10* flew past Mercury three times and sent back pictures. But the spacecraft showed us only about half the planet.

5   In March 2011, a new spacecraft named *Messenger* went around the planet again and again and again. It studied Mercury for years and finally sent pictures of the whole planet. Unfortunately, in April 2015, *Messenger* ran out of fuel and crashed on Mercury.

Planet of Extremes

6   Mercury is small. It's only 3,032 miles across. That's a bit more than the distance from New York to California.

7   Mercury speeds around the Sun in only 88 days. That's Mercury's year. So if you lived on Mercury, you'd get a birthday every 88 days.

8   But don't move there just yet. Mercury has almost no air to breathe.

9   Plus, you wouldn't like the temperature. As Mercury turns, the side that faces the Sun gets very hot ... and the other side gets very cold. Why? The Sun stays up in Mercury's sky for 88 days, raising the temperature to 800 degrees Fahrenheit (F). That temperature is hot enough to melt lead.

10 After sunset, the night lasts another 88 days, and the temperature plunges to 300 degrees F below zero. That's much colder than Earth's North Pole.

11 Mercury's surface is just as hostile. Like our Moon, it's gray and full of craters. The largest known crater on Mercury is Caloris Basin, which is 960 miles across, wider than Texas. The crater formed when a large asteroid hit the planet.

Mercury and Earth		
	Mercury	**Earth**
Average Distance from Sun	36,000,000 miles	92,960,000 miles
Year	88 days	365¼ days
Full Day (sunrise to sunrise)	176 days	24 hours
Tilt of Axis	0 degrees	23½ degrees
Diameter at Equator	3,032 miles	7,926 miles
Temperature	−300° to +800° F	−129° to +136° F
Number of Moons	0	1

Heart of Iron

12 But on the inside, Mercury differs from the Moon. In fact, it's more like Earth. Both Mercury and Earth have a core of iron.

13 "The very biggest mystery about Mercury is the origin of its large iron core," says Strom.

14 Surrounding the iron core is a rocky mantle and crust. Earth's iron core makes up one-third of Earth's mass. Mercury's iron core is a whopping two-thirds of Mercury's mass.

15 Why is Mercury's iron core so big compared with the rest of the planet? Scientists don't know. But they have some ideas.

16 Some believe that, long ago, Mercury had a thicker mantle. Then a huge asteroid hit Mercury and blasted most of the mantle away, leaving the large iron core.

17 Or maybe, long ago, the Sun blazed more brightly. The light might have vaporized most of the rocky mantle.

18 From the data collected by *Messenger*, scientists hope to shed some more light on Mercury's iron core.

19 Motions inside that core generate a magnetic field. So if you took a compass to Mercury, it would work just fine. In contrast, it wouldn't work on Venus, Mars, or the Moon, because they don't have magnetic fields the way Mercury and Earth do.

Ice on Mercury?

20 In 1991, astronomers looked at Mercury's poles and made a surprising discovery. They found what seems to be water in the form of ice.

21 How can ice exist on such a hot planet? The ice probably huddles inside craters that never see sunlight. So the ice doesn't melt. In early 2015, *Messenger* discovered water ice inside the craters of Mercury's North Pole. *Messenger* also discovered that Mercury actually shrank in width over time!

One Discovery: Volcanoes!

One of *Messenger's* discoveries in its early days included volcanoes on the surface of Mercury!

"In the past, Mercury has been very volcanically active," says planetary scientist Robert Strom. Billions of years ago, these volcanoes erupted and their lava partially covered some of Mercury's craters. However, the volcanoes probably don't erupt today.

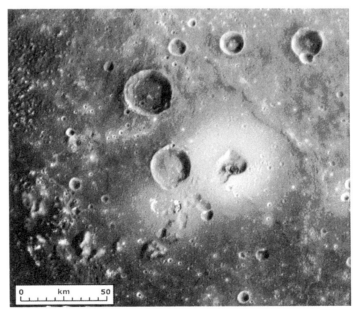

The *Messenger* spacecraft found this huge volcano. Scientists think Mercury's volcanoes are extinct.

Directions: Answer the following questions. If you need more space to write an answer, write your answer on your own paper.

1 Which two features compared in the table on page 223 best explain why Mercury's high temperature is much greater than Earth's?

A   Average Distance from Sun and Full Day

B   Average Distance from Sun and Number of Moons

C   Diameter at Equator and Tilt of Axis

D   Diameter at Equator and Year

2 The photograph on page 225 of the volcano on Mercury supports the idea that Mercury's surface is most like the surface of—

A   the Moon.

B   the Sun.

C   Venus.

D   Earth.

3 Which feature of Mercury explains why a compass would work on the surface of the planet?

A   It does not have a moon.

B   It orbits the Sun.

C   It has an iron core.

D   It has volcanoes on its surface.

4 Which of these facts about Mercury is explained in the table but not in the article?

A   Year

B   Tilt of Axis

C   Temperature

D   Diameter at Equator

5 Which evidence does the author include in the article to support the idea that people wouldn't want to move to Mercury?

   A The core of the planet is similar to the core of Earth.

   B The largest crater on the planet was caused by a large asteroid.

   C The planet appears to have water in the form of ice at its poles.

   D The planet can be hot enough to melt lead or colder than the North Pole.

6 Which sentence(s) from the article would make the best caption for the picture in the section "One Discovery: Volcanoes!"?

   A Mercury is the closest planet to the Sun, and much of it is unexplored.

   B Mercury's surface is just as hostile. Like the Moon, it's gray and full of craters.

   C But on the inside, Mercury differs from the Moon. In fact, it's more like Earth.

   D Mercury's iron core is a whopping two-thirds of Mercury's mass.

7 Based on the main article and the section titled "One Discovery: Volcanoes!," the reader can conclude that *Messenger* was more successful than *Mariner 10* because it—

   A sent back pictures of Mercury.

   B flew past Mercury three times.

   C showed us about half of Mercury.

   D showed us most of Mercury's surface.

8 Which two facts from the table on page 223 comparing Mercury and Earth would be easier to understand with a diagram?

   A Year and Number of Moons

   B Full Day (sunrise to sunrise) and Temperature

   C Average Distance from Sun and Diameter at Equator

   D Average Distance from Sun and Full Day (sunrise to sunrise)

9 Compare the missions of *Mariner 10* and *Messenger*. Explain why *Messenger* is expected to gather more information than *Mariner 10* did.

10 Identify the evidence the author includes in the "Planet of Extremes" section to show that Mercury is a planet of extreme temperatures. How does the wording the author uses to present the facts emphasize the extreme high and low temperatures? Use **two** details from the article to support your answer.

11 The author compares Mercury with places in the United States several times. Why does the author include these comparisons? Include examples of **two** comparisons in your answer.

12 Why is Mercury's iron core so large compared to the rest of the planet? Summarize the **two** theories that might explain this. Use details from the passage in your response.

13 Why does the author include the section titled "One Discovery: Volcanoes!"? How does this section relate to the rest of the article?

14 The chart in the article provides facts that show some of the differences between Mercury and Earth. Identify **two** differences that you think could be better shown by using a diagram instead of a table. Explain why you chose those differences.

15 Write an essay in which you describe how the Messenger spacecraft may solve some of Mercury's mysteries. Describe at least **two** mysteries in your answer and explain how the Messenger spacecraft could or did solve them. Use information from the article to support your answer.

Planning Space

You can complete the chart below to help plan your answer.

Mercury's Mysteries

Examples of Mysteries	How the Messenger Spacecraft Could Solve the Mystery
1)	1)
2)	2)
3)	3)

_____

_____

_____

_____

_____

_____

_____

_____

_____

_____

_____

_____

Directions: Read the passage. Then answer the questions that follow it.

My Favorite Fruit? The Olive!

By Andrea Vlahakis

1   I love plums, and I love blueberries. But as delicious as they are, my favorite fruit is—the olive!

2   The first time I ever saw olive trees was when I visited my grandmother in Greece. She lived in the Peloponnesian peninsula, in the deep south of Greece.

3   I couldn't believe that trees could look so old. Really big gnarled trunks seemed out of place with delicate, slim, silver-green leaves. Fossilized olive leaves, found in Greece, date back almost forty thousand years. I didn't know how old the trees I saw were, but they looked as if they were part of a magical forest from a thousand years ago—at least!

4   How old do olive trees really get? In the right climate—like the Mediterranean, with hot, dry summers and mild winters—anywhere from five hundred to fifteen hundred years.

Olives and My Greek Family

5   Olive orchards had been in my grandmother's family for generations. They grew Kalamata olives. Everyone worked in the orchards—parents, grandparents, brothers, and sisters. Even my father worked there.

6   As a boy in Greece in the late 1920s, my father remembers working with his *papouli*, or

grandfather, in the family's orchards. My father helped harvest the olives in late fall, when they turned from an unripe green to purplish black. The workers would lay huge tarps on the ground, then shake the olive branches with sticks to make the ripe olives fall. After harvest-time my father would help his *papouli* prune the trees for the next season.

All About Olives

7   Nothing was wasted. The pruned wood and any dead branches were used for heating. My father carried small branches home by the armfuls.

8   Some of the crop was saved to be cured and eaten. My father remembers that he and his friends used to stuff their pockets with olives to snack on while they walked to school.

9   But the family's olives were also used for oil. First, the olives were pitted and chopped. Then the olive meats were put in a press to squeeze out the oil. My father and his friends visited the presses to watch. The meats left in the press were used to feed the animals. My father remembers that the family's pigs and chickens *loved* olive meats.

10   And the oil? It was used for cooking in place of butter. During World War II, when there was little food, the Greeks ate *bobota*, a cake-like bread made from cornmeal and, you guessed it, olive oil!

11   The oil was also rubbed into the skin to keep it soft, and a few drops in just-washed hair acted as a good conditioner. My grandmother even made her own soap from the oil. It was light brown with a faint aroma of olives.

Olives and Light

12   My grandmother didn't use candles. She put olive oil in a glass with a little water. (Oil is lighter than water and floats to the

top.) She had a cork disk, the size of a quarter, with a hole in the middle, where the wick would go. The hole was edged with metal so the cork wouldn't burn. To make an olive-oil candle, she'd float the disk in the oil and then light the wick. When the oil was used up, the water put out the flame!

Olives have a strong connection to light and to Greece. The Olympic Games began in ancient Greece. It is said that a burning olive branch was the first Olympic flame.

13 As you can see, the olive is a very determined fruit from a practically indestructible tree. It has provided food, light, and heat for centuries. Plums and blueberries may be delicious, but give me olives any day.

Harvesting, Processing, and Curing Olives

14 Today in Greece, from November to mid-March, olives are harvested much the same way they were in my father's day. Yes, some people use machine harvesting, which shakes the trunks and branches. But a lot of people don't. Why? Some of the groves are very old and are on rocky land where machines can't reach. And handpicking guarantees that the olives won't be damaged.

15 The process of getting oil from the olive isn't that much different, either. But the methods are more modern. First, the olives are crushed with mechanical steel grindstones. Then, the meats are spun in a centrifuge at very high speeds to separate the oil from the meats.

16 What about the olives that you eat? You wouldn't want to eat fresh olives because they taste very bitter. They have to be *cured*, or soaked in a saltwater solution (brine), for up to six months. (The brine is changed from time to time.) Olives can also be stored in the brine.

Directions: Answer the following questions. If you need more space to write an answer, write your answer on your own paper.

1 Reread the first paragraph of the article.

> *"I love plums, and I love blueberries. But as delicious as they are, my favorite fruit is—the olive!"*

How does the rest of the article relate to the main idea of this paragraph?

A It provides support to explain why the author has this opinion.

B It compares and contrasts plums, blueberries, and olives.

C It explains why people in different countries have different tastes.

D It describes the health benefits of different types of food.

2 The illustration on page 234 is included mainly to represent—

A the age and history of the olive trees in the orchard.

B the large amount of olives produced every season.

C the hard work required to harvest the olives each year.

D the family enjoying working together in the olive orchard.

3 Which of the following would be best to include to summarize the information in the first paragraph of "Olives and Light"?

A timeline

B table

C diagram

D graph

4 Which sentence from the article supports the author's opinion that the olive is the best fruit?

A "My father helped harvest the olives in late fall, when they turned from an unripe green to purplish black."

B "My father remembers that the family's pigs and chickens loved olive meats."

C "It was used for cooking in place of butter."

D "It has provided food, light, and heat for centuries."

5 How does the first illustration on page 234 help the reader understand the article?

   A It shows how olives are grown.

   B It shows how the olives are used.

   C It shows how the olives are eaten.

   D It shows how the olives look.

6 The information in paragraph 9 could also be presented in a/an—

   A chronological list.

   B chart.

   C bar graph.

   D Venn diagram.

7 Which section provides the best support for the idea that olive growing has changed little over the years?

   A Olives and My Greek Family

   B All About Olives

   C Olives and Light

   D Harvesting, Processing, and Curing Olives

8 Which source would most likely provide more information for a report on growing olives?

   A An atlas

   B A cookbook

   C A newspaper

   D An encyclopedia

9 Reread paragraph 3 of the article. Explain how the author makes the trees seem ancient. How does this relate to the information in "Olives and My Greek Family"? Use at least **two** details from the article to support your answer.

10 How has modern machinery changed how olives are harvested? Use details from the main article and from "Harvesting, Processing, and Curing Olives" to support your answer.

11 Explain how olives are cured and why curing is necessary. Use at least **two** details from the article to support your answer.

12 As well as being used for food, olives were used for other purposes. Complete the diagram below by describing some of the other uses for olives.

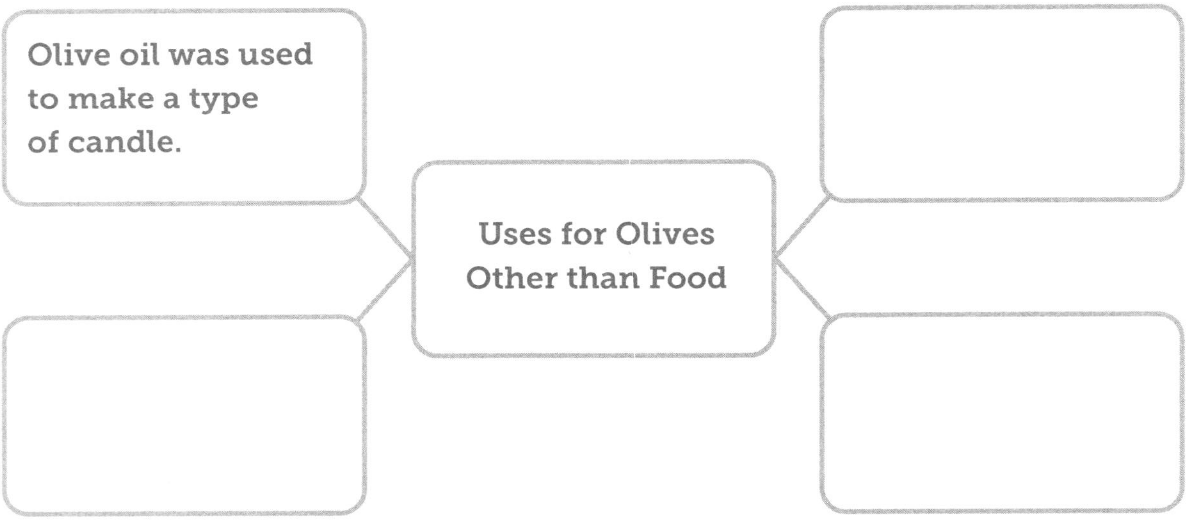

Olive oil was used to make a type of candle.

Uses for Olives Other than Food

13 In the section "All About Olives," the author states that "nothing was wasted." Which **two** details from this section best support that statement? Explain why you chose those details.

14 How does the author emphasize that growing and using olives is a family activity? Give at least **two** examples from the article to support your answer.

15 The author states at the beginning and end of the article that plums and blueberries are delicious. What is the main feature of olives that makes them better than plums and blueberries? Write an essay in which you explain what benefits olives have compared to other fruits. Use information from the article to support your answer.

Planning Space

You can complete the graphic organizer below to help plan your answer.

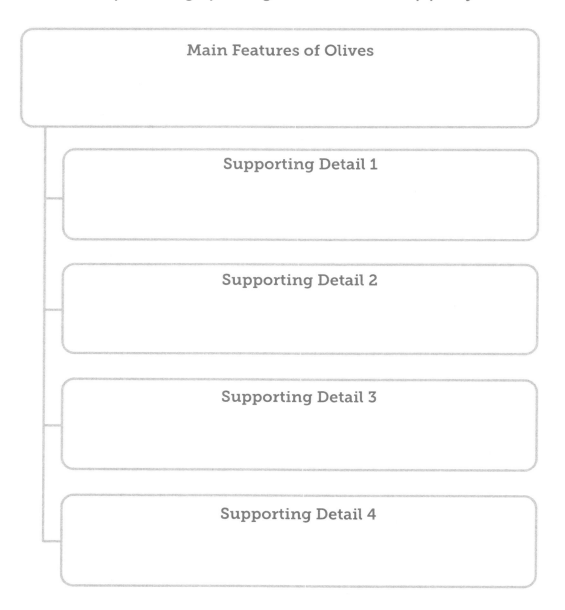

Main Features of Olives

Supporting Detail 1

Supporting Detail 2

Supporting Detail 3

Supporting Detail 4

_____

_____

_____

_____

_____

_____

_____

_____

_____

_____

_____

_____

Part D:

All Together

Literary, Informational, and Paired Passages with Multiple Choice, Short Response, Extended Response, and Essay Questions

Reading Standards

The questions in Part D cover the standards in all three sections of the standards.

Key Ideas and Details: R.4.1, R.4.2, R.4.3

☑ Informational   ☑ Literary

Craft and Structure: R.4.4, R.4.5, R.4.6

☑ Informational   ☑ Literary

Integration of Knowledge and Ideas: R.4.7, R.4.8, R.4.9

☑ Informational   ☑ Literary

Directions: Read the passage. Then answer the questions that follow it.

Benny Benson and the Flag Contest

By Martha Whitmore Hickman

1   In Alaska in January, darkness comes early. By the time Benny Benson left school, the stars were already beginning to come out in the night sky.

2   All the way home Benny thought about the contest. His teacher had announced to Benny's seventh-grade class a contest to design a flag—for the whole territory of Alaska. The contest was open to students from seventh grade through high school.

3   The year was 1927. Alaska had been a territory of the United States for more than 14 years and under the U.S. flag for almost 60 years. Now Alaska would have a flag of its own.

4   Benny looked up at the sky. He remembered how his mother had pointed out these same stars when he was a little boy far away from here.

5   Until Benny was three, he and his family had lived in Chignik, a small fishing village in Alaska. Then his mother died, and because his father was a fisherman and had to be away for weeks at a time, Benny went to live at the Jesse Lee Mission Home on the island of Unalaska. During summer, the fields were covered with blue forget-me-nots. In the windy cold winter, some of the villagers lived in cozy *barabaras*, houses dug into the ground with sod for roofs. Then the Home moved to Seward, where there were cows to milk, berries to pick, and trees—and up above, the same stars shining.

Creating His Flag

6   After supper, in his room in the Jesse Lee Mission Home, Benny got out paper and pencil, crayons and paint.

7   What could he draw that would show the Alaska he loved?

8   He thought about the long days of summer, when green plants and flowers grew and only the tops of the mountains still glittered with snow.

9   He thought of the winter, when darkness lasted from late afternoon until after breakfast the next day, when the stars shone brightly in the cold night sky, and when everyone bundled up in fur parkas, mukluks, and mittens.

10   Perhaps he should draw a high mountain, like the mountains around Unalaska or those circling Resurrection Bay? Maybe something about the great bears that trundled around the countryside? Or the tiny blue forget-me-nots that dotted the meadows in spring and summer? Perhaps the deep blue of the Bering Sea, with its fish and its fleets of fishermen? Or the high dome of the sky, with the same stars his mother had pointed out to him when he was a small boy.

11   Slowly, he began to draw. First, he drew the seven stars of the Big Dipper. Then he remembered his mother saying, "Follow the line of the Dipper's outer side, and you'll find the North Star." He drew the North Star.

12   He colored the stars as bright a gold as he could mix. He colored the background the deepest blue.

13   Then he wrote:

> *The blue field is for the*
> *Alaska sky and the forget-me-not,*
> *an Alaskan flower.*
> *The North Star is for the*
> *future state of Alaska, the*
> *most northerly in the*
> *union. The Dipper is for*
> *the Great Bear—symbolizing*
> *strength.*

14 In school, he handed in his design.

Entering the Contest

15 Each local area was to send its best entries to the capital in Juneau. The prize was to be a gold watch with the winning design engraved on the back. The winner wouldn't be announced for several months.

16 The hours of darkness remained long. The weather cold.

17 Winter deepened. Snow fell.

18 Benny and the other children went sledding and tobogganing.

19 Then March came, and vegetation began to grow on the low slopes of the mountains.

The Winner Is Announced

20 One day in March, a messenger brought a telegram to the Jesse Lee Mission School. The superintendent brought it to Benny's seventh-grade classroom and handed it to the teacher.

21 Benny and the others watched as the teacher opened the telegram.

22 She gasped and tried to speak, but she couldn't.

23 The superintendent read the telegram to the class:

> *Flag design by Benny Benson,*
> *Jesse Lee Mission School,*
> *Seward, first place*
> *unanimously. Letter follows—*
> *George A. Parks,*
> *Governor, Territory of Alaska.*

24 The boys and girls jumped from their seats, cheering and shouting. "Benny won! Benny won!"

25 Benny Benson had won the contest!

26 Benny turned pale. His heart pounded. He was too surprised to speak.

27 The whole school was excited about Benny's winning. The superintendent called off classes for the rest of the day.

28 Of course Benny was thrilled that he had won. He was glad, too, when it was time for "lights out" and he could go to the quiet of his room and think about what had happened.

29 For the rest of his life, Benny Benson would be honored as the person who designed the Alaskan flag—which many have called the most beautiful flag of all.

Directions: Answer the following questions. If you need more space to write an answer, write your answer on your own paper.

1 What is the main purpose of the article?

   A to describe what the Alaskan flag looks like

   B to describe how the Alaskan flag was created

   C to explain why Alaska did not have a flag until 1927

   D to compare the flag of Alaska to the flags of other states

2 Which paragraph is included mainly to show that Benny Benson achieved something great?

   A Paragraph 26

   B Paragraph 27

   C Paragraph 28

   D Paragraph 29

3 Read these two pairs of sentences from the passage.

   Benny looked up at the sky. He remembered how his mother had pointed out these same stars when he was a little boy far away from here.

   First, he drew the seven stars of the Big Dipper. Then he remembered his mother saying, "Follow the line of the Dipper's outer side, and you'll find the North Star."

   Which of the following describes the connection between these two pairs of sentences?

   A Both show how the stars reminded Benny of his mother.

   B Both explain how Benny felt about flags.

   C Both hint that Benny liked to study the stars.

   D Both suggest that Benny felt lonely.

4 The author mostly organizes this passage by—

A describing a problem Benny has and offering a solution.

B presenting events in the order they happen to Benny.

C explaining why Alaska needed a flag.

D comparing different parts of Alaska.

5 Which of these presents the best summary of the story?

A Benny liked many things about living in Alaska. He liked the blue flowers that appeared in summer. He liked the bright stars that appeared in the winter sky.

B Benny lost his mother when he was young. His father was a fisherman, so Benny went to live at the Jesse Lee Mission Home. He went to school near there and played with his friends.

C Benny wanted to enter a contest to design a flag for Alaska. He thought about the stars that shine in the night sky. He drew a picture of a blue flag with stars. Benny's design won the contest.

D Benny thought about the contest. He thought about drawing the great bears that lived in the countryside. He thought about drawing a picture of the blue sea. Finally, he drew a picture of stars.

6 Which idea is supported by the information in the section "Creating His Flag?"

A Benny put a lot of thought into his design.

B Benny was shocked that his design had won.

C Benny was remembered for his design for a long time.

D Benny added stars to his design because he enjoyed winter.

7 The author mostly uses paragraph 5 to—

A show how Benny decided on a design.

B describe the places where Benny lived.

C describe the things Benny enjoyed doing.

D show that Benny had few ideas for a design.

8 How were stars important to Benny as a child? Explain what stars meant to him. Use details from the article to support your answer.

9 In paragraph 10, the author asks a series of questions. Explain why the author asks these questions. How does asking questions relate to the main idea of the paragraph? Use details from the article to support your answer.

10 Complete the chart below by describing **three** features of the Alaskan flag. Explain what each feature represents.

Main Features of the Alaskan Flag

Feature	Meaning

11 Compare the reactions of Benny, his teacher, and his classmates to Benny winning the contest. Who seems most shocked by the win? Use at least **two** details from the article to support your answer.

12 The telegram quoted in paragraph 23 uses the word *unanimously*, which means "agreed on by everyone." What does the use of the word show about the success of Benny's design? Use details from the article to support your answer.

13 How does quoting Benny's words in paragraph 13 support the idea that Benny thought carefully about his design? Use details from the article to support your answer.

14 The author includes descriptions of the seasons throughout the article. Explain why the author includes these descriptions. Use at least **two** examples from the article to support your answer.

Planning Space

You can write notes, make a list, or draw a chart to help plan your answer.

15 The article begins with two paragraphs that read like a story. What is the most likely reason the author started the article this way? How might this help readers relate to the article? Use details from the article to support your answer.

Planning Space

You can write notes, make a list, or draw a chart to help plan your answer.

Directions: Read the passage. Then answer the questions that follow it.

The View from Camp

By Clare Mishica

Dear Mother and Dad,

1. My roommate, Syd, may be a problem. He's so sloppy it looks like ten duffel bags exploded in our cabin. He whistles real loud through this gap in his front teeth, too. Plus, he knocked over our lamp and broke it. Syd also wears a funny blue hat for good luck, but I don't think it's working.

Love,
Bryan

Dear Mom and Pop,

2. My roommate, Bryan, seems kind of jumpy, like our cat when you turn on the vacuum cleaner. He hung up a big poster of all the constellations, so maybe he'll teach me how to find them. I'm sure we'll be best buds. Guess what? Our cabin got a brand new lamp.

Love,
Syd

Dear Mother and Dad,

3. Don't worry, but today I almost drowned. We went canoeing across the lake to have a picnic on an island. Halfway there, Syd spotted this fish in the water and dropped his paddle. Before it floated away, I leaned over to grab it, then Syd leaned over, too. We tipped our canoe, and our lunch sank into the muck on the bottom. It felt like I was floating in a giant cup of iced tea! Everything got soaking wet—except for Syd's hat. The other

campers let us borrow some extra clothes, and I had to wear an itchy purple sweatshirt. Syd picked some blueberries for us. He's OK, but I'm probably going to get pneumonia.

Love,
Bryan

Dear Mom and Pop,

4   Today I saw this enormous fish while we were canoeing. The counselor said it might have been a northern pike. I got a real close look before I fell in the lake. My life jacket worked great, and I bobbed up like a cork. The other campers shared all their clothes and food, so I got to meet everyone. Now I have new friends from seven different towns! I'll write more later—I have to help hang up our wet clothes. Bryan has been in a very soggy mood.

Love,
Syd

Dear Mother and Dad,

5   Syd attracts trouble like my giant magnet grabs paper clips. We went for a hike, and Syd stepped on a wasps' nest. The wasps were not happy. The counselor grabbed Syd's hand, and they raced down the trail. The rest of us ran the other way. I got two blisters from running, and poor Syd got stung twice on his face. He said his lucky hat helped him swish most of the wasps away, but that hat mostly brings bad luck. Now Syd has huge chipmunk cheeks. Of course, he can still whistle, but I don't mind anymore.

Love,
Bryan

Dear Mom and Pop,

6   I plan to join the cross-country team this fall. Today I ran half a mile in about three and a half minutes. The counselor said my legs pumped faster than the pistons in his car engine. The wasps that were chasing us probably helped a little. Did you know that some wasps make their nests on the ground? Dad, will you help me train for cross-country when I get home?

Love,
Syd

7   PS: I heard Bryan whistling along with me yesterday. Last night, he showed me the Big Dipper and Orion. Then we made up a new constellation and named it Wasper. We laughed so hard we got the hiccups.

Dear Mother and Dad,

8   Tonight we had a talent show. Syd and I tried to act out *Jack and the Beanstalk*, but Syd accidentally pulled down our rope beanstalk. Everyone laughed, and I wanted to do a disappearing act. Then Syd started telling the campers about our week, and he threw me his lucky hat to act out the stories. Pretty soon, the room was

roaring, and we won first place. Maybe Syd's hat is lucky after all. I had it on last night, and a bunch of campers came to visit. Syd told them I'm a pro with constellations, and they wanted me to point them out. I never made so many friends at one time. I didn't even mind the mess they made in our cabin. I can't believe this, but I'm going to miss Syd.

Love,
Bryan

Dear Mom and Pop,

9   The talent show was fantastic. Bryan really got into it, and we won first place. I may try out for the junior-high play next spring. The counselor told me that I'm a natural onstage and terrific at improvising. At first, I thought that meant yanking down ropes, but it really means making stuff up as you go along.

10   Camp has been the greatest. I was sad to start packing. When Bryan wasn't looking, I put my lucky hat in his bag. He really likes it now, and I want him to have it. Besides, I'm lucky without a hat! See you soon.

Love,
Syd

Directions: Answer the following questions. If you need more space to write an answer, write your answer on your own paper.

1 What does the word *view* in the title most likely refer to?

   A   how two people saw things that happened

   B   how one person ruined the camp for another

   C   how the camp was in a beautiful setting

   D   how the camp taught people to do new things

2 In paragraph 5, Bryan describes Syd's "huge chipmunk cheeks." What does Bryan mean by this?

   A   Syd could not stop laughing about what happened.

   B   Syd started blushing because he was embarrassed.

   C   Syd had swollen cheeks from the wasp stings.

   D   Syd keeps telling jokes about the wasps.

3 Both Bryan and Syd describe the same events in their letters. How do their letters differ from each other?

   A   Bryan's letters express sadness while Syd's letters express happiness.

   B   Bryan's letters discuss only the bad while Syd's letters discuss only the good.

   C   Bryan's letters take a serious approach while Syd's letters take a silly approach.

   D   Bryan's letters make camp seem dull while Syd's letters make camp seem interesting.

4 In paragraph 4, Syd describes Bryan as "soggy" to suggest that Bryan is—

A boring.

B damp.

C gloomy.

D tired.

5 Which of these best explains how Bryan and Syd's feelings about each other change throughout the story?

A From friendly to cold

B From uncertain to accepting

C From hopeful to disappointed

D From jealous to understanding

6 All of these sentences suggest that Syd likes having new experiences EXCEPT—

A "He hung up a big poster of all the constellations, so maybe he'll teach me how to find them."

B "My life jacket worked great, and I bobbed up like a cork."

C "I plan to join the cross-country team this fall."

D "I may try out for the junior-high play next spring."

7 What lesson can the reader learn from reading this story?

A Good things come to those who wait.

B A true friend sees past a person's faults.

C Think about what could happen before acting.

D What a person is like on the inside counts most.

8 Reread paragraphs 1 and 2 of the story. What main detail about the new lamp does Syd leave out of his account? What is the most likely reason he leaves it out? Use details from the story to support your answer.

9 Paragraphs 3 and 4 describe the canoeing accident. How is the tone of Syd's account different from the tone of Bryan's account? What does this suggest about what each character is like? Use details from the story to support your answer.

10 A simile is a comparison of two things using the word *like* or *as*. Identify **two** similes Bryan uses in his letters. Explain why Bryan uses each simile.

11 Syd can be described as someone who only sees the best in things. How does Syd's letter describing the wasps illustrate this? Use details from the story to support your answer.

12 How does Bryan feel when things at the talent show first go wrong? How do his feelings change by the end of the talent show? Use details from the story to support your answer.

13 Look closely at the illustration on page 260 showing the canoeing accident. How can you tell which character is Bryan and which is Syd? Explain what you can tell about how they each feel about falling out of the canoe.

14 How does Bryan feel about Syd's whistling at the beginning and end of the story? Explain how the whistling is used to show Bryan's changing feelings towards Syd. Use details from the story to support your answer.

Planning Space

You can write notes, make a list, or draw a chart to help plan your answer.

_____

_____

_____

_____

_____

_____

_____

_____

_____

_____

_____

_____

_____

15 A main theme of "The View from Camp" is that there are two sides to every story. How does the structure of the story help communicate the theme? Use details from the story to support your answer.

Planning Space

You can write notes, make a list, or draw a chart to help plan your answer.

Directions: Read the passage. Then answer the questions that follow it.

Crimson Harvest: A Visit to a Cranberry Farm

By Judith Boogaart

1   When winter blows icy cold from the north, Loren House floods his cranberry bogs with water from his small lake. The cranberry vines rest underwater through the long winter. A crust of ice keeps them safe from wind, frost, and snow. But when spring comes and the ice turns to mush and melts, the cranberry bogs come to life.

2   Loren House uses weather forecasts and years of farming know-how to decide when to drain the bogs. Too soon, and a late frost could kill the tender buds. Too late, and the roots would not get the oxygen they need to grow.

3   The thick mat of vines turns reddish brown over the winter. Loren prunes back any old, woody, or overgrown vines before the new shoots appear. Then he feeds them with fertilizer.

4   Soon the sun coaxes the vines to send up new shoots. These short *uprights* sprout shiny green leaves but will not bear fruit this year.

5   In June, buds on last year's shoots open, and the bogs become a carpet of pink-white flowers.

6   Every day, bees buzz among the flowers collecting nectar. The pollen they carry

The Bitter Berry

When Pilgrims first landed in Massachusetts, some of the Algonquin people who lived there shared food with them. Cranberries grew wild in the bogs along the shore, and the natives called them *ibimi*—"bitter berry." When the Pilgrims saw the vines in bloom, the shape of the flowers reminded them of a familiar bird, the crane. They called the fruit "crane-berries," which later became "cranberries."

from blossom to blossom starts the berries growing. When the blossoms fade and drop, the berries begin to appear as little green hubs called *pinheads*.

Tending the Bogs

7   Taking care of the bogs keeps Loren House busy. He checks the spongy soil and irrigates when it is too dry. He weeds out grasses and sedges. He uses a net to sweep the vines for cranberry fruit flies and beetle grubs and decides how to control them. He chooses the best treatment for diseases like root rot and leaf spot.

8   Loren House learned cranberry farming from his father and grandfather. His great-uncle bought this land in 1876, and the family has farmed here ever since. Most cranberries grow in New England, Wisconsin, or the Northwest, but this part of Michigan also has what they need. Winds blowing across Lake Superior keep the weather warmer in winter and cooler in summer. The vines like the sandy, acidic soil. And there is plenty of fresh water to irrigate and flood the bogs.

9   Over the next few weeks, the pinheads grow as big as peas and then marbles. They change color from green to pink to red. By October, the berries are crimson, ripe, and ready to pick.

Harvesting the Berries

10   Harvesting is hard work. Some berries are dry harvested. Loren House walks a machine through the dry beds. It has *tines*, like those on a fork. They *comb* the berries off the vines into a box at the back of the machine. The berries then go into a separator. Its blower removes loose vines and leaves. Berries fall down onto small shelves called *bounce boards*. Bad, mushy berries don't bounce; they slide off the shelves to the ground. Only good, firm berries bounce down the shelves to a long tray for final sorting, cleaning, and bagging by hand. Loren House and his wife, Sharon, sell these fresh at their store.

11 Loren House also uses a method called wet harvesting. First he floods the bog until water covers the plants. Then he drives a water-reel harvester through the bog. Its fat tires don't harm the plants. A big reel churns up the water and loosens the berries from the plants. The berries float to the top of the water because they have pockets of air in their centers.

12 Wearing high-wading boots, Loren House and his helpers use floating *boom boards* to gently drag the berries toward a conveyor. His grandsons gather stray berries with butterfly nets.

13 Trucks carry the berries to a machine on the farm for first cleaning. Then they are loaded on big trailers and shipped to another cleaning station and on to the processor.

14 There they become the juice and sauce that show up on our tables.

15 Soon the December winds will howl again. Time for Loren House to put the cranberry bogs to bed for another winter, the way his family has been doing for more than 100 years.

Directions: Answer the following questions. If you need more space to write an answer, write your answer on your own paper.

1 What does the word *crimson* in the title of the article refer to?

   A   where cranberries got their name from

   B   where the cranberries are grown

   C   what cranberries taste like

   D   what cranberries look like

2 All of the following sentences support the idea that the cranberry farm is a family business EXCEPT—

   A   "Loren House uses weather forecasts and years of farming know-how to decide when to drain the bogs."

   B   "Loren House learned cranberry farming from his father and grandfather."

   C   "Loren House and his wife, Sharon, sell these fresh at their store."

   D   "His grandsons gather stray berries with butterfly nets."

3 Throughout the main article, the words in italics are meant to show words that—

   A   relate to cranberry farming.

   B   come from another language.

   C   should be read with more force.

   D   are most important to the article.

4 Which words from paragraph 7 help the reader understand the meaning of the word *irrigates*?

   A when it is too dry

   B uses a net

   C sweep the vines

   D how to control them

5 Which sentence from the article would make the best caption for the photo of the cranberry bog?

   A "When winter blows icy cold from the north, Loren House floods his cranberry bogs with water from his small lake."

   B "He uses a net to sweep the vines for cranberry fruit flies and beetle grubs and decides how to control them."

   C "Wearing high-wading boots, Loren House and his helpers use floating boom boards to gently drag the berries toward a conveyor."

   D "Trucks carry the berries to a machine on the farm for first cleaning."

6 What can the reader learn from the shaded box titled "The Bitter Berry" that cannot be learned from the main article?

   A the color of cranberry flowers

   B how cranberries got their name

   C the steps for harvesting cranberries

   D how to protect cranberries in winter

7 Which of these best describes the organization of paragraphs 11 through 14?

   A They offer solutions to a problem.

   B They list a sequence of events in order.

   C They describe the effects of a given cause.

   D They explain how things are alike and different.

8 The article describes how the bogs are drained each year. Why is it important that the bogs are drained at the right time? Use details from the article to support your answer.

9 The section "Harvesting the Berries" describes how bounce boards are used in the harvesting. Explain how the bounce boards sort the berries. Use details from the article to support your answer.

10 Read this sentence from the last paragraph of the article.

"Time for Loren House to put the cranberry bogs to bed for another winter, the way his family has been doing for more than 100 years."

Explain what the author means by "put the cranberry bogs to bed." Use details from the article to support your answer.

11 The section titled "Tending the Bogs" tells how Loren House has to solve problems to keep the cranberry plants healthy. Complete the graphic organizer below by describing **two** problems and how they are solved.

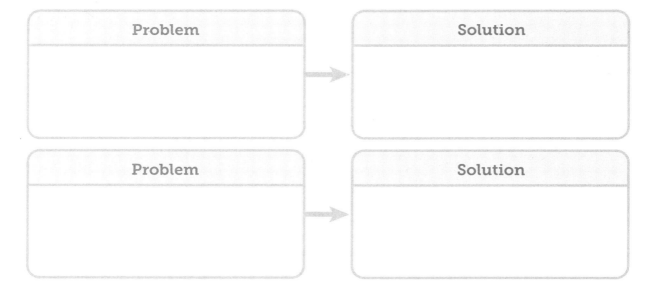

Problem		Solution

Problem		Solution

12 What does the section "The Bitter Berry" describe? Explain why the author included this section. Use details from the article to support your answer.

13 The photograph on page 274 shows a process described in the article. Use details from the article to write a summary of the process shown.

14 In "Harvesting the Berries," the author states that "harvesting is hard work." Does the author include enough details to support this statement? Use details from the article to support your answer.

Planning Space

You can write notes, make a list, or draw a chart to help plan your answer.

15 The cranberries can be harvested by dry harvesting or wet harvesting. Compare how the berries harvested each way are used. Why do you think the berries harvested each way are used for different purposes? Use details from the article to support your answer.

Planning Space

You can write notes, make a list, or draw a chart to help plan your answer.

Directions: Read the following two passages. Then answer the questions that follow.

Ready

By James Price

1   Five seconds to go.
    Two points behind.
    Standing just beyond
    the three-point line.

2   Should I call for it?
    What if I miss it?
    Can I do it?

3   "Here! Here!"
    The ball is mine.
    The chance is mine.
    The game could be ours.

4   No time to think.
    Just shoot.
    My body acts
    while my mind races.

5   The ball soars
    towards the net.

6   Bodies pause in mid-step.
    Faces turn in slow motion.
    Silence.

7   It sails through.
    Three points.
    The win.

8   My team cheers.
    The other team sighs.
    "Lucky shot," someone mumbles.

9   No. Not luck.
    Hours of work.
    Hours of practice.
    Hours preparing for one moment.
    And I was ready
    for that moment.
    I did it.
    I don't remember how
    but I did it.

Making a Lay-Up

By Anthony F. Stump

1   The lay-up is the most basic shot in basketball. Professional players have to make lay-ups at full speed with defenders trying to block the shot. But you can practice alone, as long as you know how to do it.

2   When you practice a skill enough times, it becomes automatic. To make a lay-up, you'll be jumping off one foot while shooting with the opposite hand. Your shooting hand will be the one farther from the basket, making it difficult for a defender to block the shot.

3   The best way to learn a skill like this one is to break it into smaller steps, learning to shoot the ball first and then adding footwork and dribbling.

The Angle Shot

4   Stand to the right of the basket, about three feet away. With your elbow bent, hold the ball in your right hand. Lift that hand so it's next to your head with the palm up. Tilt your wrist backward and let the ball rest on the pads of your fingers, not in your palm. Steady the ball with your left hand and bend your knees. Keep your eyes on the square on the backboard. Aim for the top corner of the square (the side closest to you) and launch the ball. Your goal is to bank the ball into the basket by bouncing it off the backboard.

Step and Shoot

5   Stand about six feet from the basket this time and take a large step with your left foot. That foot will land about where you were standing for the angle shot. As your left foot reaches that spot, jump off it and make the shot with your right hand. (You'll

be bending your right knee as you jump.) That's how to make a right-handed lay-up.

Footwork

6   After you've mastered the one-step lay-up, move several feet farther back. Dribble with your right hand. Make your last step with your left foot, jumping up and forward with that foot and taking the shot with your right hand. At first, you might need to take a few short steps in order to reach the proper spot for the left-footed jump. Practice dribbling slowly, then increase your speed as you get the hang of it. The faster you approach the basket, the "softer" your shot needs to be.

Double Your Skill

7   You can use these same steps for left-side lay-ups, but use the opposite hand and foot. Jump with the right foot and shoot with the left hand.

8   By learning to shoot from both sides and with both hands, you'll become a much more effective player.

9   Remember that you can improve most athletic skills by thinking about the action. Picture yourself making a lay-up with proper form, jumping off the correct foot. The more you practice, the easier it will be for your brain to remember. Soon you'll be doing it automatically.

10   Now go practice!

Directions: Use "Ready" to answer the following questions. If you need more space to write an answer, write your answer on your own paper.

1 What do the lines in the second stanza represent?

A things that people in the crowd yell

B what the speaker worries about

C how the other players make the speaker feel

D questions the coach asks of the players

2 Which line best helps the reader imagine how nervous the speaker feels?

A "The chance is mine."

B "No time to think."

C "while my mind races."

D "The ball soars"

3 "Ready" is an example of which kind of poetry?

A Haiku, a short poem about nature

B Limerick, a nonsense poem for children

C Free verse, a poem without a set rhyme or meter

D Epic, a long poem about the adventures of a hero

4 The lines in stanza 2 of "Ready" suggest that the speaker feels—

A disgusted.

B prepared.

C strong.

D unsure.

5 How is the poem different from prose? What features show that "Ready" is a poem? Use details from the poem to support your answer.

6 What is the purpose of the poem "Ready?" Does the first-person point of view help the poem achieve its purpose? Use details from the poem to support your conclusion.

7 Read the following lines from "Ready."

"Bodies pause in mid-step.
Faces turn in slow motion."

What are these lines describing? How do the two lines show how the players feel? Use details from the poem to support your answer.

Directions: Use "Making a Lay-Up" to answer the following questions. If you need more space to write an answer, write your answer on your own paper.

8 The boy in the illustration on page 286 in "Making a Lay-Up" is making the shot described under which heading of the article?

A The Angle Shot

B Step and Shoot

C Footwork

D Double Your Skill

9 The author uses subheadings to divide the information into sections. Describe how the sections "The Angle Shot," "Step and Shoot," and "Footwork" fit together. Use details from the article to support your answer.

10 The article shows that it takes practice to perfect a lay-up. Using information from the article, explain why it would be worthwhile for a player to perfect the shot. Use at least **two** reasons to support your answer.

11 Is the main purpose of the passage to instruct, inform, or encourage? Use details from the article to support your answer.

Directions: Use both "Ready" and "Making a Lay-Up" to answer the following questions.

12 Which sentence from "Making a Lay-Up" supports the theme of "Ready"?

A "But you can practice alone, as long as you know how to do it."

B "Practice dribbling slowly, then increase your speed as you get the hang of it."

C "The more you practice, the easier it will be for your brain to remember."

D "Now go practice!"

13 Both the author of "Making a Lay-Up" and the speaker in "Ready" believe that—

A teamwork is necessary for success.

B practice is the only way to improve.

C winning is the most important thing.

D giving respect leads to getting respect.

14 Read these sentences from the end of "Making a Lay-Up."

> *"The more you practice, the easier it will be for your brain to remember. Soon you'll be doing it automatically."*

How do these sentences relate to the speaker in the poem? Use details from the poem and the article to support your answer.

Planning Space

You can write notes, make a list, or draw a chart to help plan your answer.

_____

_____

_____

_____

_____

_____

_____

_____

_____

_____

_____

_____

15 The poem and the article are both about practicing basketball skills. Compare how each passage shows the importance of practicing. Which passage do you think would most make a player want to practice new skills? Use details from the poem and the article to support your answer.

Planning Space

You can complete the chart below to help plan your answer.

	Ready	Making a Lay-Up
How are the ideas presented?		
How does it show the importance of practicing?		
Would it make players want to practice?		

Directions: Read the passage. Then answer the questions that follow it.

Going in Circles Around Saturn

By Ken Croswell, Ph.D.

1   Saturn is spectacular, boasting bright and beautiful rings. You can see the rings through a telescope.

2   The edge of the outside main ring is a huge circle 170,000 miles across. That's nearly three-fourths of the distance from Earth to the Moon. But the rings are just 30 feet thick. You could walk such a short distance in a few seconds.

3   The rings are made of trillions of ice particles going around Saturn. Some of the ice particles are as small as marbles; others are as big as horses and houses.

4   Saturn is the Sun's only planet with brilliant rings. Jupiter, Uranus, and Neptune also have rings, but their rings are dark and hard to see. All of these planets are giants, much larger than Earth.

What Made the Rings?

5   Where did Saturn's rings come from? People have wondered for hundreds of years, ever since astronomers discovered the rings.

6   But now Robin Canup, Ph.D., may have solved the puzzle. She's a scientist at the Southwest Research Institute in Boulder, Colorado, and she uses computers to see what happens when planets and moons interact with one another.

7   Dr. Canup thinks Saturn's rings formed when a big moon smashed into the planet.

Planets Rock!

8   Dr. Canup became interested in astronomy long ago. "Back in second grade, part of our science book was on the Moon and the planets," she says. "I liked thinking about whether there were other planets that might have life on them."

9   There's no life on Saturn.

10 The planet is too far from the Sun and too cold. But Saturn was her favorite planet. "It is stunningly beautiful," she says.

11 Saturn has more than just incredible rings. It also has 62 moons, or satellites. They go around Saturn just as the Moon goes around Earth. One of Saturn's moons, named Titan, is bigger than our Moon. Titan is even bigger than Mercury and Pluto. Many of Saturn's moons, including Titan, formed in a disk of gas and dust that went around Saturn billions of years ago, when Saturn was young.

A Possible Solution

12 Dr. Canup thinks she can solve the mystery of Saturn's rings. She has an interesting idea, or hypothesis, about how the rings formed.

13 She thinks that once, long ago, Saturn had another large moon just like Titan. After the Titan-like moon formed, it spiraled through the disk of gas and dust, moving closer and closer to Saturn, until the moon crashed into the planet.

14   Like Titan, the moon was half rock and half ice. The rock was at the moon's center. The ice was on the surface.

15   "As the moon got very close to Saturn, the gravity of Saturn was strong enough to begin to strip material from it," Dr. Canup says.

16   That's because gravity causes tides. A tide occurs when gravity pulls harder on one side of an object than on the other side. For example, the Moon's gravity pulls Earth's seas up and down.

17   In the same way, Saturn's tides yanked on the big moon's ice. As the moon moved closer to Saturn, it passed through the Roche limit. The Roche limit is where a planet's tides tear things to shreds.

18   "So Saturn's gravity stripped ice from the satellite," says Dr. Canup. "The planet started peeling off the outer layers of the satellite, but the satellite was continuing to spiral inwards." Dr. Canup thinks the ice particles went into orbit around Saturn and became the rings.

Plunging into Saturn

19   However, Dr. Canup says, Saturn's tides didn't tear up the moon's rocky core. Because rock is denser than ice, the core resisted Saturn's tides. The rock plunged into Saturn. In the moon's place were glorious rings of ice, with almost no rock.

20   Dr. Canup's idea agrees with all the laws of planetary motion. But to test her idea, she needs to study more planets with big, bright rings.

21   Giant planets go around many stars besides the Sun. Maybe some of those planets have rings as spectacular as Saturn's. If so, then Dr. Canup may be able to see whether their rings were made by large moons that crashed into their planets.

The Birth of Saturn's Rings

Where did Saturn's spectacular rings come from? Dr. Canup's idea may solve the mystery.

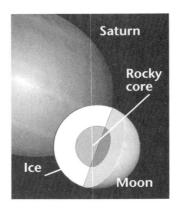

Billions of years ago, Saturn was bigger than it is today. Dr. Canup thinks it had an icy moon with a rocky core.

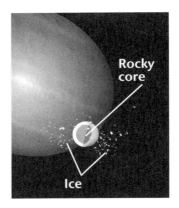

If such a moon crossed the Roche limit, Saturn's powerful gravity would have peeled off the moon's ice layer.

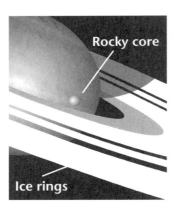

Trillions of ice pieces would have gone into orbit around Saturn, forming wide, flat rings.

The rocky core of the moon would have plunged into Saturn, leaving the rings behind.

Directions: Answer the following questions. If you need more space to write an answer, write your answer on your own paper.

1 Read this sentence from the article.

> *"After the Titan-like moon formed, it spiraled through the disk of gas and dust, moving closer and closer to Saturn, until the moon crashed into the planet."*

What does the word *spiraled* suggest about the moon?

A   It shone brightly.

B   It moved slowly.

C   It was out of control.

D   It was hard to see.

2 According to the article, how will Dr. Canup find evidence to support her theory?

A   by observing Saturn's largest moon, Titan

B   by studying other planets with bright rings

C   by comparing the rings of all the giant planets

D   by collecting data on Saturn using computers

3 How are the rings of Jupiter, Uranus, and Neptune different from Saturn's rings?

A   They are older.

B   They are wider.

C   They are dimmer.

D   They are rockier.

4 The author organizes paragraphs 2 through 4 mostly by—

A   comparison and contrast.

B   problem and solution.

C   chronological order.

D   cause and effect.

5 Which sentence from the article suggests that Dr. Canup's idea about how Saturn's rings formed is correct?

   A   Dr. Canup thinks she can solve the mystery of Saturn's rings.

   B   In the same way, Saturn's tides yanked on the big moon's ice.

   C   In the moon's place were glorious rings of ice, with almost no rock.

   D   Dr. Canup's idea agrees with all the laws of planetary motion.

6 The author most likely included the diagram to—

   A   help readers understand Dr. Canup's idea about Saturn's rings.

   B   explain why Dr. Canup thinks Saturn is so beautiful.

   C   show readers what Saturn's rings look like.

   D   compare Saturn to other planets.

7 A telescope allows people to see things in outer space. Based on this, the prefix *tele-* most likely means—

   A   across.

   B   distance.

   C   large.

   D   measure.

8 What effect does the Moon's gravity have on Earth?

   A   It tears the ice off objects.

   B   It pulls objects to the ground.

   C   It creates the tides in the seas.

   D   It makes rings around the planet.

9 Paragraph 3 explains that Saturn's rings are "made of trillions of ice particles." How does this fact support Dr. Canup's theory? Use details from the article to support your answer.

10 How are the author's and Dr. Canup's feelings about Saturn similar? Use at least **two** specific details from the article to show how the author and Dr. Canup feel about Saturn.

11 Reread paragraph 3 of the article. Explain why the author compares the ice particles to marbles, horses, and houses. Use details from the article to support your answer.

12 In the section "Planets Rock!," the author quotes Dr. Canup. Explain the purpose of the quotes and describe the background information they give. Use details from the article to support your answer.

13 The third diagram in "The Birth of Saturn's Rings" refers to the Roche limit. Explain what the Roche limit is. What is the difference between a moon orbiting outside the Roche limit and a moon orbiting inside the Roche limit? Use details from the article to support your answer.

14 The last diagram in "The Birth of Saturn's Rings" shows how the rocky core plunged into Saturn. What does the diagram show about what happened when the rocky core hit Saturn? How does this explain why there would not be rock in the planet's rings? Use details from the article to support your answer.

15 The diagrams on page 298 are included to show how Saturn's rings formed. Using the diagrams as a guide, write a summary of the events that occurred to form Saturn's rings. Use information from the diagrams and the main article in your answer.

Planning Space

You can complete the chart below to help plan your answer.

How Saturn's Rings Formed

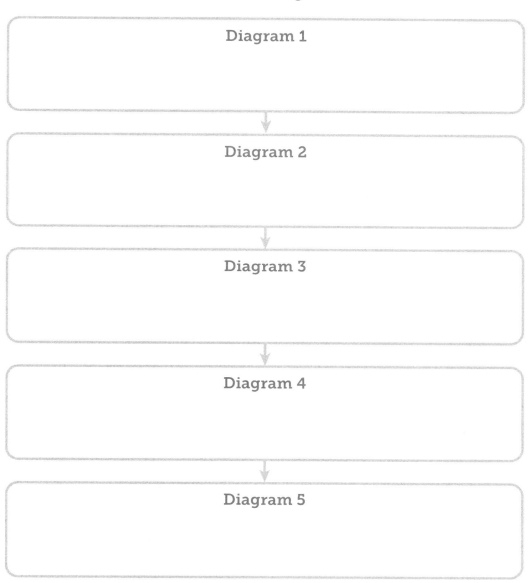

Diagram 1

Diagram 2

Diagram 3

Diagram 4

Diagram 5

_____

_____

_____

_____

_____

_____

_____

_____

_____

_____

_____

_____

_____

_____

Directions: Read the following two passages. Then answer the questions that follow.

Little Mo

By James M. Janik

1   Montgomery Ashford got his nickname back in sixth grade.

2   While the rest of us doubled in size the summer before middle school, Little Mo still had to sit on his feet to see at the movies. When we'd take turns jumping for the rim during basketball in gym class, Little Mo needed a boost to nick the net with a fingertip. Little Mo was, well, little.

3   Most guys would waste their time whining about such a lousy break. It's tough to fit in when you're looking up at everyone's chin most of the time. Little Mo never complained. In fact, he saw his shortness as a positive. He was funny that way. Once you knew him and how he saw things, it was impossible to feel sorry for him.

4   For most of the year, especially during football and basketball seasons, Little Mo avoided attention. Keeping "under the radar" is what he called it. When March rolled around, things changed. Little Mo lived for the spotlight of baseball season.

5   At the start of the first game, the opposing team slung the usual insults. Little Mo just smiled. All the kids on our bench folded their arms, waiting.

6   After the pitcher and catcher finished their giggling and snickering and got down to the business of pitching, their smirks faded.

7   Little Mo dug in the batter's box, the sleeves of his jersey hanging down past his elbows.

8   Now, the typical strike zone is a nice big rectangle. Home plate is 17 inches wide, and most 12-year-olds have a workable distance between their knees and their armpits. When Little Mo crouched, his rectangle seemed to fold up like a road map. From the pitcher's mound, Little Mo's strike zone looked like a mail slot.

9   The catcher squatted as low as he could, but his mitt still made too high a target. He tried lying down but couldn't find any place to stick his fingers to call pitches. Finally, he kneeled on the ground and hoped he wouldn't have to go anywhere in a hurry.

10   The pitcher squinted, searching for some reasonable place to throw the ball. But there was no reasonable place. Little Mo got his walk on four pitches every time he was up. He dropped his bat and ran to first base.

11   Little Mo's height advantage didn't stop there. You might think running fast on such short legs would be impossible. But you'd only think that if you never saw a millipede zip across the kitchen floor or a chipmunk dash from the flower bed to the weed line. Short legs make for small steps, but short steps take less time to make.

12 Giving up a walk to Little Mo was the same as giving up a triple. The next hitter only had to watch two pitches go by, and Little Mo would steal second, then third. Before the pitcher knew what had happened, Little Mo would be standing on third, waiting to score.

13 Little Mo set all sorts of league records. He started every All Star game. He was a run-scoring machine.

14 By the end of the season, we all wished we weren't quite so tall. Our strike zones were enormous! It took forever for our long legs to carry us to second base on a steal.

15 Little Mo grinned whenever we mentioned how lucky he was to be so short and fast. He agreed that he was lucky to get so much attention but never rubbed it in. He was funny that way.

16 His luck ended the year he turned thirteen.

17 Little Mo went off to summer camp right after our last game. As always, he'd led the league in walks, steals, and runs scored. When he came back from camp, he'd grown six inches. His voice had dropped about three octaves. We didn't recognize him. His mom called it a growth spurt. We called it a disaster. We'd lost the best lead-off hitter in the league's history! What a lousy break.

18 But Little Mo didn't see it like that. He said he'd always wanted to give basketball a try. And he thought he might like to try wide receiver, too. We just scratched our heads. He was funny that way.

Fishing for Gold

By Teresa Bateman

1 Everyone agreed that Eamon was the laziest leprechaun in all of Ireland.

2 While other leprechauns were cobbling, playing the harp, dancing, or practicing magic, what was Eamon doing? Fishing! Who ever heard of a leprechaun that fished?

3 Since fishing took up all his time, Eamon couldn't make a shoe, play a tune, or dance a jig. And magic? Well, that was a complete disaster.

4 The other leprechauns shook their heads.

5 "You need to practice harder."

6 "You need to study harder."

7 "You need to try harder."

8 But Eamon didn't want to. He loved to fish, and he was good at it. He had only to cast his line and fish came leaping to his bait.

9 "It's a tasty talent," his friends said, laughing, "but magic can put food on the table with less effort. And it's magic you'll need to be a true leprechaun."

10 Eamon knew that this was so. Soon he'd be given a pot of gold. Gold strengthened leprechaun magic, and according to law each leprechaun of a certain age had to guard a pot of it.

11 The safest place to hide this leprechaun gold was at the end of a rainbow—where only leprechaun magic could reach. Unfortunately, Eamon's magic was so weak, he couldn't get to the end of a rainbow.

12 "You need to practice harder."

13 "You need to study harder."

14 "You need to try harder."

15 So he did. He cobbled ill-fitting shoes, strummed his harp while the neighbors held their ears, and stepped on the toes of any partner willing to risk a dance with him.

16 And he practiced magic. But he couldn't get the magic to work.

17 To raise his spirits, Eamon walked to the brook one sunlit morning. He cast his fishing line as he cast his mind in search of a solution. Then, gazing at his favorite waterfall, he suddenly knew what to do.

18 The day arrived to go before the throne.

19 "This is leprechaun gold," the king said solemnly, placing the gleaming pot before Eamon. "Can you keep it safe?"

20 The young leprechaun nodded. "I will place it at the end of a rainbow and retrieve it when there's need."

21 After the ceremony, Eamon hid his gold.

22 Summer arrived— the hottest one Ireland had known. The skies were steely blue with nary a cloud, and the grass withered on the hills.

23 With no rain, there could be no rainbows. With no rainbows, it was impossible for the leprechauns to reach their treasure.

24   As the days of drought continued, magic in the community faded. The leprechauns grew thinner, for magic had helped put food on their tables. Eamon's fishing became more than a hobby as he began feeding his friends and neighbors.

25   Dry days turned to dry weeks. Then one day a sentry came running into the village square.

26   "There are men in our valley!" he cried.

27   Usually this would have been a small problem. The leprechauns would use magic to lead the men away, but their magic had worn thin as a thimble.

28   Eamon knew what he had to do. He hurried to the king's throne and bowed. "Might leprechaun gold help?"

29   The king frowned. "Gold would help, but how can we find the end of a rainbow without rain?"

30   Eamon hesitated. "I hid my gold, as I said."

31   The king nodded.

32   "I'd better show you," Eamon continued.

33 The king followed Eamon to the waterfall. "You didn't hide it at the end of a rainbow trout, did you?" he joked.

34 Eamon chuckled nervously, then pointed. Smaller due to the drought, the waterfall still sent out enough spray for the sun to spread a rainbow in the mist. Eamon reached in and pulled out his pot of gold.

35 The king smiled. "You're a clever leprechaun. You followed the law, in your own way, and it's lucky you did. Your gold can keep everyone safe until the rains return."

36 So he said, and so it was. Each leprechaun took a gold coin from the pot. Together, they used their magic to befuddle the intruders. The village was safe again.

37 There was a great celebration—a fine fish dinner, of course.

38 Eamon continued to share his gold and his fish until the rains fell. Nobody laughed at him anymore, and everyone came to him for fishing lessons.

39 Few, however, were willing to put in the time and energy fishing required.

40 "You need to practice harder, study harder, and try harder," Eamon told them, but he said it with a twinkle in his eye. "Well, we all have our talents. Go ahead and chase your rainbows. Just let me chase mine in my own way."

Directions: Use "Little Mo" to answer the following questions. If you need more space to write an answer, write your answer on your own paper.

1 What do the details in paragraph 3 mainly show about Little Mo?

A He gets upset easily.

B He does not stand up for himself.

C He has a good sense of humor.

D He is relaxed and easygoing.

2 The author describes Little Mo as a "run-scoring machine." What does the word *machine* mainly suggest?

A Little Mo scores runs without thinking.

B Little Mo is good at scoring runs.

C Little Mo scores runs the same way every time.

D Little Mo is tired of scoring so many runs.

3 The narrator of the story helps the reader understand Little Mo mainly by—

A describing his actions.

B quoting his speech.

C telling his emotions.

D showing his problems.

4 Read these sentences from paragraph 5 in "Little Mo."

At the start of the first game, the opposing team slung the usual insults. Little Mo just smiled. All the kids on our bench folded their arms, waiting.

The last sentence suggests that the kids—

A are impatient for their turns at bat.

B think they are better baseball players.

C know something the other team does not.

D are not friends with the players on the other team.

5 How would "Little Mo" be different if it were written in the first person?

  A It would use a lot of dialogue.

  B It would include stage directions.

  C It would include Little Mo's thoughts.

  D It would describe Little Mo's appearance.

6 Look closely at the illustration of Little Mo and the catcher on page 306. Describe how Little Mo and the catcher seem to feel. How does this support information in the story? Use details from the story to support your answer.

7 Read these sentences from paragraph 8 of the story.

  "When Little Mo crouched, his rectangle seemed to fold up like a road map. From the pitcher's mound, Little Mo's strike zone looked like a mail slot."

Are the similes an effective way to emphasize how hard it was to pitch to Little Mo? Use details from the story to support your answer.

Directions: Use "Fishing for Gold" to answer the following questions. If you need more space to write an answer, write your answer on your own paper.

8 Read these sentences from "Fishing for Gold."

"You need to practice harder."

"You need to study harder."

"You need to try harder."

Why does the author most likely repeat these lines throughout the story?

A   To prove that Eamon is not actually lazy

B   To emphasize the pressure Eamon feels

C   To explain how Eamon feels about himself

D   To show that Eamon does not have friends

9 Read this sentence from paragraph 19 of "Fishing for Gold."

"This is leprechaun gold," the king said solemnly, placing the gleaming pot before Eamon.

The word *solemnly* most closely means—

A   kindly.

B   peacefully.

C   quietly.

D   seriously.

10 Why is the lack of rain important in the story? How does it lead to Eamon needing to use his talents? Use details from the story to support your answer.

11 Read this dialogue spoken by the king.

> *"You're a clever leprechaun. You followed the law, in your own way, and it's lucky you did. Your gold can keep everyone safe until the rains return."*

How does this dialogue summarize the main lesson of the story? Use details from the story to support your answer.

12 At the beginning of the story, the other leprechauns think Eamon is lazy. How does the view of Eamon change by the end of the story? What causes their views to change? Use details from the story to support your answer.

13 Read these sentences from the last paragraph.

"You need to practice harder, study harder, and try harder," Eamon told them, but he said it with a twinkle in his eye.

What does the phrase "with a twinkle in his eye" show about Eamon? What can you infer about how he feels? Use details from the story to support your conclusion.

Directions: Use both "Little Mo" and "Fishing for Gold" to answer the following questions.

14 What message do "Little Mo" and "Fishing for Gold" share?

A Everyone is special in his or her own way.

B Always be ready to try something new.

C Look to others when you need help.

D Being honest is always best.

15 Everyone has both strengths and weaknesses. Think about how Little Mo and Eamon each have strengths and weaknesses. Write an essay in which you describe how the characters Little Mo and Eamon both show the importance of being yourself and making the most of who you are. Use information from both stories to support your answer.

Planning Space

You can complete the chart below to help plan your answer.

	Little Mo	Eamon
Strengths		
Weaknesses		
Using Strengths and Weaknesses		

_____

_____

_____

_____

_____

_____

_____

_____

_____

_____

_____

_____

_____

_____

_____

_____

_____

_____

_____

_____

_____

_____

_____

_____